I0142339

SEEKING
TREASURES

DONNA E. LANE, PH.D.

Copyright © 2019 by Donna E. Lane
All rights reserved. No part of this book may be reproduced in any manner whatsoever without written permission.

Unless otherwise indicated, all Scripture quotations are taken from THE HOLY BIBLE, NEW INTERNATIONAL VERSION®, NIV® Copyright © 1973, 1978, 1984, 2011 by Biblica, Inc.® Used by permission. All rights reserved worldwide.

ISBN 978-1-7328112-7-0

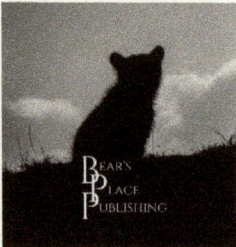

BEAR'S PLACE PUBLISHING
SNELLVILLE, GEORGIA, USA

Contents

Acknowledgements   6
Dedication   7

THE MAP   9

ONE: THE TREASURE OF IDENTITY
    Your Compass   17
    Map Key: The Outflow of Your True Nature   19
    Starting Point: Questions to Explore Identity   36
    Destination: Prayers to Uncover Identity   38
    Setting the Course: Living Your Identity   41

TWO: THE TREASURE OF AUTHORITY
    Your Compass   45
    Map Key: Agency, Ownership, and Choice   47
    Starting Point: Questions to Explore Authority   64
    Destination: Prayers to Uncover Authority   65
    Setting the Course: Living Your Authority   68

THREE: THE TREASURE OF INDWELLING
    Your Compass   73
    May Key: Never Alone   75
    Starting Point: Questions to Explore His Indwelling 94
    Destination: Prayers to Uncover His Indwelling   95
    Setting the Course: Living in His Indwelling   99

FOUR: THE TREASURE OF PROTECTION

Your Compass 103
May Key: Sword and Shield 105
Starting Point: Questions to Explore His Protection 125
Destination: Prayers to Access His Protection 126
Setting the Course: Living in His Protection 129

FIVE: THE TREASURE OF SANCTIFICATION

Your Compass 133
Map Key: Evidentiary Exclusion 135
Starting Point: Questions to Explore Sanctification 155
Destination: Prayers for Spiritual Maturity 156
Setting the Course: Living in His Sanctification 159

SIX: THE TREASURE OF WISDOM

Your Compass 163
Map Key: Discerning Costume Jewelry 165
Starting Point: Questions to Explore Wisdom 185
Destination: Prayers for Wisdom 186
Setting the Course: Gaining God's Wisdom 189

SEVEN: THE TREASURE OF FREEDOM

Your Compass 193
Map Key: Purchasing the Field 195
Starting Point: Questions to Explore Freedom 213
Destination: Prayers for Freedom 214
Setting the Course: Living in Freedom 218

EIGHT: THE TREASURE OF THE KINGDOM
    Your Compass   223
    Map Key: Pearls of the Kingdom   225
    Starting Point: Questions on Kingdom Living   247
    Destination: Prayers for Kingdom Living   248
    Setting the Course: Living in the Kingdom   251

CONCLUSION   256

Definitions   258
Resources   259

Acknowledgements

I wish to thank my husband, David Lane, for his support, encouragement, insight, and patience. You are Bjorn Shieldbearer to my Helga Anna, Hamish to my Braveheart, Samwise to my Frodo, Han Solo to my Leia, Captain Kirk to my Spock. My love and my strength, my split-apart on this temporal plane, words cannot express my love and appreciation.

I also wish to acknowledge the invaluable contributions of Andie Newell and Connie Mitchell, who offered feedback and editing prior to publication.

I also wish to acknowledge and thank the countless individuals who have nurtured me on my treasure quest and who continue to provide fellowship and support as my quest continues.

Most of all, I wish to thank my son, Cody, who now lives in the Kingdom, his quest completed. Your example of someone who sold everything to purchase the true treasures of God gives me hope for my own quest to come to an end with hearing the words, "Well done, good and faithful servant," for I'm certain your quest did. You are a treasure in the lives of the many people you touched, and the wonder and beauty of your true nature continues to usher the Kingdom into the world.

Dedication

For Coen and Petra

I wrote this book for you, so you would always have a map to follow to live the Kingdom life, to flow in your best, true self to the fullest expression of your identity in Christ, to know your authority, to experience His indwelling Spirit and His protecting presence, to revel in your sanctification, to make your life choices in God's wisdom, and to understand and live in the true freedom provided in love by Jesus.

The Map

"The kingdom of heaven is like treasure hidden in a field. When a man found it, he hid it again, and then in his joy went and sold all he had and bought that field. Again, the kingdom of heaven is like a merchant looking for fine pearls. When he found one of great value, he went away and sold everything he had and bought it."

Life is a quest. We are all created to be seekers.

Evidence of our searching nature is reflected in the epic stories we write and love to read (or watch). In the best stories, the hero or heroine goes through great hardship, overcomes many obstacles, and defeats the enemy, and ultimately, they complete their quest and discover the treasure they seek. We are drawn to these types of stories because they reflect God's narrative design of our lives.

The nature of our individual quests is determined by what we deem valuable in our lives. Jesus puts it this way: "For where your treasure is, there your heart will be also" (Matthew 6:21). At our best, we actively choose the treasure we seek and pursue our quest with purpose and intent. At our worst, we are swept up in the

9

ebb and flow of circumstances, distractions, enemy deceptions, and unconscious motivations, and our seeking drives us away from the very things we desire in our true hearts.

Certainly, some quests are more noble than others, some more beneficial than others, and some more meaningful than others, but, according to Jesus, seeking His Kingdom is the only quest that consummately matters: the treasure hidden in the field; the pearl of unmatched value (Matthew 13:44-45). God provides us with a map to His Kingdom in Scripture. Through parables about the Kingdom of God and His other teachings, Jesus reveals the nature, qualities and characteristics, and locus of His great treasures. Through the example of His life, He demonstrates how to discover and obtain His treasures.

This book will draw together all the resources found in Scripture to build a treasure map, a guide for pursuing a quest for the Kingdom of God. Along the way on our quest, we will encounter great beauty. We will build up our strength and expose our weakness and need. We will discover partnership and fellowship. We will acquire weapons for the inevitable confrontation with our enemy. We will slog through valleys where darkness reigns, and we will soar above the world to reach new heights in our understanding. We will gain wisdom, knowledge, insight, and truth that will serve us well in the battle. We will learn reliance on new ways, and we will allow our old ways to perish. And at the end of our quest, we will decide if we will choose to sell all we have to purchase the treasures we have found.

Reading a map requires several steps. The first step is, of course, choosing the right kind of map for what you are seeking, then orienting your map properly to ensure you are examining it from the correct perspective so you can get your bearings. A map contains a compass rose to show you how to orient your map toward true north. The "compass rose" for each chapter of this book will be grounding Scripture, which will orient you toward the treasure for that section and center your perspective on truth. I will refer back to the grounding Scripture and other, related verses, throughout the chapter.

The second step in map reading is understanding the Map Key (also known as the legend). The Map Key helps you make sense of the map. It shows the topography of the map and explains the symbols and meanings of the elements of your map. For this book, the "Map Key" will be a discussion of the concepts, ideas, symbols, and meanings of the verses used to describe the treasure you seek. This discussion will help you interpret and navigate the map as you seek the treasure.

Once you have a "true north" orientation and an understanding of the "Map Key," you must identify your location and destination. To find where you are going, you must know where you are beginning your quest. Each chapter will provide questions to help you determine your "location" spiritually, to help you find your starting point on the quest. Next, you will need to pinpoint your destination. You will never complete your quest if you don't know where you are going. For each chapter, I will present ideas for prayers and meditations, to assist you in understanding where you want to end up and the work it may take to reach your destination.

The final step in reading a map is setting your course. Looking at your starting point and destination, you choose which roads or paths you want to take to get from Point A to Point B. Usually, the best route is the most direct one, with minimal detours.

Each chapter will provide possible action steps for walking out the path to your destination. Your exact course will be one of your choosing, but I hope to provide options and alternatives from which you may choose. Unfortunately, a map cannot alert you to road closures and other obstacles, so I will identify some potential obstacles you may encounter and ways to respond to those obstacles should you face them.

Each section is designed to take a week to complete, but be flexible with the process, taking as much time as needed to fully receive everything the Lord has for you in your quest.

Begin by reading the Scripture verse, your "Compass Rose" for the section. Many of the verses may be familiar to you, but take time to read them anew, not just by rote, and consider how each verse reveals some specific aspect of the Kingdom of God. Take the time to look up each verse and read the sections surrounding the selection to see the context. Ask what the Lord is wanting to say to you in those verses. Prayerfully, look deeper than the obvious or surface meaning, because the Holy Spirit can breathe new revelation and understanding each time we open our hearts to His truth.

Next, read the discussion, your "Map Key" for the section. You may want to read through it once, then go back over it a second time more deliberately, focusing on any points that bring up questions for you or lead to new insights. I suggest having a notebook to use with this study to write down any questions you have as they arise. You can also use it to take notes on the key points you want to remember.

Once you feel you have fully absorbed the ideas presented in the discussion, answer the questions provided along with any questions that came up for you during the reading. These questions are designed to help you identify your "Starting Point" on your quest and integrate truths about His treasures deeply into your heart until they become part of your regular thoughts, feelings, and perspectives.

After you answer the questions, set aside time to spend in prayer with the Lord. The suggested prayers provide possible directions to reach your "Destination." Allow substantial time for listening for His responses to your prayer questions. This process may take several days. Don't rush your process. You may focus on one question at a time, or you may choose to have a lengthier "get away" for deep meditation and prayer where you wait in solitude to hear from the Lord. If you do not readily hear from the Lord, do not press to the point of feeling frustrated with the process. Instead, ask the Lord to show you what may be in the way of hearing Him, feeling His presence, or receiving His truth in your heart.

Keep in mind, part of any quest is encountering an enemy who is actively thwarting your efforts to reach God's treasure. Our enemy often tries to interfere in our attempts to hear from Jesus, specifically because in trying to hear, we are seeking God, so do not allow Satan to blame or condemn you if you do not hear readily. Jesus does speak to you and will speak to you in the way that is both most beneficial for you and most readily received by you. The Lord may bring answers to your questions at any point throughout the day or week, in a variety of ways. So, remain open to whatever and however He responds. When the Lord speaks to your heart in response to your seeking Him, follow wherever He leads you; do not feel you must rigidly follow the questions provided in the book, as they are suggestions only and may or may not be relevant to what the Lord wants to reveal to you.

13

"Setting Your Course" at the end of each section provides applications that build one upon another to develop a three-dimensional, detailed map for seeking God's treasures. The goal is for you to grasp concepts, not develop a list of steps to take or rules to follow. If you understand the concepts, you will be able to see the whole "map" so you can choose the route you want to take to apply the information presented in the chapter to your life.

First, process the information you have gleaned from each section by internalizing the elements you want to adopt. You may use the ones provided and add your own based on your takeaways. Take each concept and include it as a point of focus for your quest. Then, process the information by applying the concepts through action. These applications give suggested ways to use your treasure map, based on the elements you choose to adopt. Be intentional and specific in how you apply the concepts to your daily life; however, remember, these applications are not a list of steps to follow. Instead, think of the process as a rucksack of tools you can carry with you on your quest and a cache of weapons you can use in battle, and choose your actions based on which tools and weapons work for you.

Finally, consider creating a sketch of the "map" uncovered in the chapter (think creatively and illustrate what you've gained from the section in a way that is meaningful to you, using drawing, painting, images, or any other form of artistic expression), so by the end of the study, you can piece together the entire "map" as you understand it. Don't worry if you are not artistically inclined; creating a work of art isn't the point. Your "map" may simply be lines on a page connecting related ideas, or a chart listing key concepts you want to be sure to remember. The goal is to create a map you understand and are able to follow in your daily life.

As you move through each chapter of the book, continue to use earlier elements of your treasure map as you add new pieces. Constantly add to your tools and weapons arsenal. At the end of the study, you will have a cohesive, three-dimensional map to the Kingdom Life that strengthens you to stand on God's truth and remain in His peace.

This book can be used as a study for small groups or classes, as a book study, or as a personal journey of exploration and growth. In whatever way it is utilized, I pray, at the end of the quest, you will find yourself more intimately connected with Jesus, more aware of who you are, more grounded and strengthened in His authority, more certain of His love for you, free from fear and shame, supremely confident in His protection, more aware and able to resist fake treasures, and well on your way in your quest for the Kingdom Life.

In this life, we are going to seek *something*. We are built for it. Jesus suggests, "Seek first His Kingdom" (Matthew 6:33). The question of our lives is: what will we choose to seek?

ONE

The Treasure of Identity

YOUR COMPASS

Through him all things were made; without him nothing was made that has been made. In him was life, and that life was the light of all mankind. (John 1:3-4)

For God, who said, "Let light shine out of darkness" made his light shine in our hearts to give us the light of the knowledge of God's glory displayed in the face of Christ. (II Corinthians 4:6)

"Do not fear, for I have redeemed you; I have summoned you by name; you are mine - everyone who is called by my name, whom I created for my glory, whom I formed and made." (Isaiah 43:1,7)

"You are worthy, our Lord and God, to receive glory and honor and power, for you created all things, and by your will they were created and have their being." (Revelation 4:11)

17

Don't you know that you yourselves are God's temple and that God's Spirit dwells in your midst? (I Corinthians 3:16)

As water reflects the face, so one's life reflects the heart. (Proverbs 27:19)

His divine power has given us everything we need for a godly life through our knowledge of him who called us by his own glory and goodness. Through these he has given us his very great and precious promises, so that through them you may participate in the divine nature, having escaped the corruption in the world caused by evil desires. (II Peter 1:3-4)

So God created mankind in his own image, in the image of God he created them (Genesis 1:27).

You have searched me, LORD, and you know me. Such knowledge is too wonderful for me, too lofty for me to attain. For you created my inmost being; you knit me together in my mother's womb. I praise you because I am fearfully and wonderfully made; your works are wonderful, I know that full well. My frame was not hidden from you when I was made in the secret place, when I was woven together in the depths of the earth. Your eyes saw my unformed body; all the days ordained for me were written in your book before one of them came to be. (Psalm 139:1, 6, 13-16)

MAP KEY: THE OUTFLOW OF YOUR TRUE NATURE

IDENTITY DEFINED

*W*ho are you?

This question could be answered in many different ways. You could describe your physical characteristics – are you a male or female? Tall or short? What color is your hair? Your eyes? Your skin? I could draw some basic conclusions about you from these descriptions, but none of them capture the essence of who you are, do they?

You could tell me what you do – are you a teacher? A lawyer? Do you work in a factory? Do you deliver the mail? You could describe your living situation – are you married or single? Do you have children? Are you wealthy, comfortable, or poor? Once again, I might make some judgments about you based on your job title or social and financial status, but I would still be missing the core of what defines you.

You could describe your personality – are you an introvert or extrovert? Do you tend to be perfectionistic? Are you stand-offish? Are you a people-pleaser? These traits tell me more about you, but I still wouldn't know the fundamental, foundational answer to the question.

If I am going to truly know who you are, I need to understand your inner qualities; in other words, the unique, intrinsic characteristics of your nature. Beyond your personality, these qualities reside in your spirit, your innermost being. They are placed in you by God at your creation. They are not a result of what you do or how you look or how you behave. They are the essence of your being. This is the definition of identity.

The first and most precious treasure God gives you is your identity. You are fearfully and wonderfully made *in His image* (Psalm 139:14; Genesis 1:27). As His child, you are created to mirror His nature. Your spirit reflects His glory. He gives your heart the capacity to love and your mind the capacity for wisdom and understanding. He is the designer of your whole being.

But beyond these general truths about identity we all share, you hold specific aspects of His reflection, "knit together" (Psalm 139:13) by God with those precise qualities for the exact time and place you are and for the life you are living. Step out of yourself for a moment and contemplate the magnificence of God, who imagined the vastness of the mountains and depths of the oceans and spread them across the planet, teeming with life; who engineered the tides and orchestrated the curve of each wave; who splashed vivid colors across the sky at sunset just to express His glory and beauty; who in each strand of DNA created a language that said, "you are a bird," "you are a crab," and "you are an elephant." God, who made and intimately knows the stars and the amoeba, the vast and the microscopic, decided He wanted a *YOU*. He wove Himself into your DNA, within the language He created to say "you are a human being, made in My image" and chose specific aspects of His nature to combine in unique ways to make a one-of-a-kind work of art that has never been seen before on this earth and will never be seen again: *YOU*. And He did this on purpose, with intent.

20

DOING OR BEING?

Before you jump to the conclusion that I'm referring to a purpose He has in mind for you to "do something" for Him or "accomplish a task" on His behalf, let me clarify. I'm not referring to a "do." I am describing a state of being. He made you exactly who you are, with the identity He chose, reflecting the aspects of His nature He put in you, for the purpose of you being you. In other words, He created you to *BE*. He desires the nature or identity He created to flow freely from you into the world. By being who you were created to be, the aspects of God's nature He wove into you are also expressed into the world.

To help you understand this concept, let's use the example of a chair. The craftsman designs the shape of the seat just so for comfort. He shapes the arms and places them at the right height to provide a resting place for hands or arms. He curves the back in such a way to give adequate support. He fills the cushions to make them soft and covers them with beautiful material to make the chair a lovely addition to home décor. He carves the legs, making them thick and sturdy enough to support weight but with a designer's flare. When all these elements come together, the chair is ready to be a chair, just by being as it was created.

Would you now tell this chair to dry someone off when they get out of the shower? Or carry someone down the road to the grocery store? Would you expect it to be a television? No. By being what it was created to be, it fulfills its purpose.

THE EXAMPLE OF JESUS

The best way for you to understand the concept of identity is to look to Jesus for His example. Since you are made in God's image, it stands to reason you can see in Jesus a complete picture of the possible qualities God used to create your identity. So, who is Jesus?

Jesus is, first and foremost, loving ("As the Father has loved me, so have I loved you" – John 15:9). He has a servant's heart ("the Son of Man did not come to be served, but to serve, and to give his life as a ransom for many" – Matthew 20:28). He is compassionate ("When he saw the crowds, he had compassion on them, because they were harassed and helpless, like sheep without a shepherd" – Matthew 9:36), and He is also fierce ("In the temple courts he found people selling cattle, sheep and doves, and others sitting at tables exchanging money. So he made a whip out of cords, and drove all from the temple courts, both sheep and cattle; he scattered the coins of the money changers and overturned their tables. To those who sold doves he said, 'Get these out of here! Stop turning my Father's house into a market!' His disciples remembered that it is written: 'Zeal for your house will consume me'" – John 2:14-17).

He is determined ("Jesus turned and said to Peter, 'Get behind me, Satan! You are a stumbling block to me; you do not have in mind the concerns of God, but merely human concerns'" – Matthew 16:23) and passionate ("Jerusalem, Jerusalem, you who kill the prophets and stone those sent to you, how often I have longed to gather your children together, as a hen gathers her chicks under her wings, and you were not willing" – Luke 13:34) and persevering ("He fell with his face to the ground and prayed, 'My Father, if it is possible, may this cup be taken from me. Yet not as I will, but as you will'" – Matthew 26:39). He is also a lover of truth, confrontational and direct ("Woe to you, teachers of

SEEKING TREASURES | DONNA E. LANE

the law and Pharisees, you hypocrites! You are like whitewashed tombs, which look beautiful on the outside but on the inside are full of the bones of the dead and everything unclean" – Matthew 23:27).

He is a leader ("My sheep listen to my voice; I know them, and they follow me" – John 10:27), and a radical, a pioneer ("You have heard that it was said, 'Love your neighbor and hate your enemy.' But I tell you, love your enemies and pray for those who persecute you" – Matthew 5:43-44). He is kind and caring ("Come to me, all you who are weary and burdened, and I will give you rest" – Matthew 11:28). He is wise, a deep thinker ("'In the Law Moses commanded us to stone such women. Now what do you say?' They were using this question as a trap, in order to have a basis for accusing him. But Jesus bent down and started to write on the ground with his finger. When they kept on questioning him, he straightened up and said to them, 'Let any one of you who is without sin be the first to throw a stone at her'" – John 8:5-7).

Jesus has a peaceful spirit ("Do not worry about tomorrow, for tomorrow will worry about itself" – Matthew 6:34). He is very open, genuine, and expressive ("'You unbelieving generation,' Jesus replied, 'how long shall I stay with you? How long shall I put up with you?'" – Mark 9:19). He is also creative ("The secret of the kingdom of God has been given to you. But to those on the outside everything is said in parables" – Mark 4:11). Finally, He is a light shining into the world ("I am the light of the world" – John 8:12).

Jesus is described this way as a child: "And the child grew and became strong in spirit" (Luke 1:80), and again, "And the child grew and became strong; he was filled with wisdom, and the grace of God was on him" (Luke 2:40), so we know from the first, Jesus was strong, wise, and filled with grace. These qualities continued into His adulthood and carried Him through the torturous ordeal of the cross. He never turned from His path, never backed down from the truth, and never strayed from His nature – "the Father is in me, and I in the Father." (John 10:38). This is the example He set for us to follow, and these are the qualities He created into us.

THE ENEMY'S TEMPTATIONS

When Jesus was tempted in the wilderness, His identity was the very thing Satan attacked.

> "Then Jesus was led by the Spirit into the wilderness to be tempted by the devil. After fasting forty days and forty nights, he was hungry. The tempter came to him and said, "If you are the Son of God, tell these stones to become bread." Jesus answered, "It is written: 'Man shall not live on bread alone, but on every word that comes from the mouth of God.'" (Matthew 4:1-4).

In this first temptation, Satan asked two questions of Jesus: 1) Are You who You say You are? 2) Are You alone on this journey? When Satan said, "*if* You are the Son of God…" he was challenging the very core of Jesus' identity and demanding Jesus prove His identity by the power of His own actions. When Satan commanded Jesus to turn the stones to bread, he was questioning if Jesus believed it was all up to Him to provide for Himself and to meet His own needs, like someone alone and uncared for. Jesus responded that He didn't need to take care of Himself, because He knew the truth ("every word that comes from the mouth of God") of His identity, and He knew He was not alone.

> "Then the devil took him to the holy city and had him stand on the highest point of the temple. "If you are the Son of God," he said, "throw yourself down. For it is written: 'He will command his angels concerning you, and they will lift you up in their hands, so that you will not strike your foot against a stone.'" Jesus answered him, "It is also written: 'Do not put the Lord your God to the test.'" (Matthew 4:5-7).

Once again, Satan started his temptation with questioning the core of Jesus' identity ("*if* you are the Son of God"), then the enemy challenged Jesus to question if He was loved. Satan's question to Jesus was: Are you loved enough for God to send angels to save you? Do you matter? Jesus answered He didn't need to test God to know the answers. He already knew He was loved.

> "Again, the devil took him to a very high mountain and showed him all the kingdoms of the world and their splendor. "All this I will give you," he said, "if you will bow down and worship me." Jesus said to him, "Away from me, Satan! For it is written: 'Worship the Lord your God and serve him only.'" Then the devil left him, and angels came and attended him." (Matthew 4:8-11).

For the final temptation, the enemy changed tactics. A direct challenge to Jesus' identity wasn't working, so Satan tried to get Jesus to base His identity on external sources. Would Jesus base His value on what He had instead of on who He was? Could He be tempted to use tangible, temporal, and worldly riches as proof of His worth? But Jesus rejected the enemy's offer and based His worth on God alone. He didn't look to external things to give Him value or to define Him.

25

You face these same temptations from the enemy. Your identity is under constant threat and can come under attack in many ways. Just as Satan tempted Jesus in the wilderness ("*if* you are the Son of God…" – Matthew 4:3, 6), Satan introduces some measurement for you to meet. He deceives you into believing you must prove your own identity and suggests comparison as a method for testing your worth. He asks, "Are you good enough?" then goes on to add, "Are you as good as…" It's as if Satan transforms himself into a measuring rod and holds up a never-ending ruler for you to use to test your value, always extending the rod farther if you dare to believe you have reached your goal.

Is this measuring rod familiar to you? Satan has used it since the beginning. He tempted Eve in the same way, telling her, *if* you eat of the fruit of the forbidden tree, *if* you go against God, then "your eyes will be opened, and you will be like God" (Genesis 3:5). He suggested she measure herself against God instead of knowing herself through knowing God. He tempted her to compare herself to God and to try to be like God; in other words, he wanted her to want to be her own god. Humankind has followed suit ever since. Satan still wants you to measure your worth and value, as if you can know your identity on your own, by using his measuring rod. However, his measurement means nothing. You can only know your true, best self – your God-given identity – in the context of your relationship with God.

Jesus is in you, and you are in Him (John 17:21-23). Your true reality exists in this self-contained, complete, and sufficient sphere with Jesus, unified and connected, sharing life in Him and with Him. Within this sphere is where you can know your true identity, without comparison or measurement – just you and Jesus together as one. Satan tries to convince you being immersed in and with Jesus is not enough, and that you need to measure against some other external standard, but anything external to your identity in Christ is a distraction and not the promised "proof" of your worth.

God created you, and your identity reflects God's nature, so comparing yourself to others and finding yourself lacking is the same as saying God is lacking – that He isn't enough. This deception is an attack on the very nature of God. When you believe Satan's lie that you are not enough, you are saying God is not enough. Believing God is enough is the basis of your trust in Him, so if you accept the lie God is not enough, you undermine your ability to trust Him. And since trust is the foundation of any relationship, this deception undermines the core of your relationship with God. Can you see the cunning strategy and the purposes for Satan planting the idea of a measuring rod? Ultimately, he is after destroying your relationship with God.

In childhood, you may be told or treated as if your identity is not good enough or is worthless and without value. Your parents may have expectations that are not in alignment with your nature. Similar to my chair analogy, if your parent asks you to be a serious-minded stoic when you are built with the heart of a free spirit, this can be very damaging to your view of your nature. Abandonment, rejection, criticism, being ignored, negativity in the environment, and abuse can instill lies about your identity in your heart, lies such as "I don't matter," "I'm not good enough," and "I'm not lovable." Do you see how Satan tried to use these same lies in his first two temptations of Jesus? You might begin to see the world as a fearful place and believe only bad things will ever happen to you. You could also begin to believe something was fundamentally wrong with you, and it was all your fault. When the seeds of these lies are planted in your heart, shame, fear, and self-loathing overtake your view of yourself.

These lies begin to act like a thick, black blanket, covering up the beauty of your created self, inch by inch and yard by yard. The seeds of lies planted in your childhood are then watered, nurtured, and reinforced by circumstances and other external factors throughout your life. You begin to look for proof text to support your belief the lies are true. Like someone who is walking through a forest, fearfully looking out for snakes and bugs, you don't notice the beauty of the sunlight glistening through the leaves or the droplets of water reflecting tiny rainbows as they fall. Instead, you are prying up rocks and searching under fallen branches and scouring the ground for slithering things, so, of course, what you notice and remember are the snakes and bugs.

In the same way, the lies you believe become a lens through which you interpret your experiences. An acquaintance doesn't speak to you at a group gathering, which you perceive as evidence no one likes you, even though in reality, the individual simply didn't see you. Your boss gives you suggestions for improvement at your annual evaluation, and you hear her saying you are worthless and a failure, when she actually intended to give you encouragement because she believes in your abilities. Your child pitches a temper tantrum at the grocery store, and you're convinced he doesn't love you, when he is only testing limits like all children do.

As time goes on and you continue to interpret your experiences through the lens of your lies, the roots of those lies go deeper and the black blanket gets thicker and heavier. Other painful experiences of life, which are a natural part of living in this fallen world, add to the oppressive mix to strengthen the beliefs. The deeply rooted lie beliefs can eventually hide your true identity completely, so when you try to look at yourself, you see only the thick blanket of lies that now feel true to you.

Because the enemy can't steal your identity from you, because it is written into the DNA of your body, soul, and spirit, he settles for covering up your identity under the blanket of lies. His attempts to hide your identity and keep it from flowing into the world accomplish much the same outcome as robbing it from you. Your purpose, which is to allow your unique nature to express freely into your sphere of influence, is thwarted if your identity is hidden.

In Satan's second temptation of Jesus, you can see another enemy strategy used to attack your identity, something extremely prevalent in today's culture: the postmodern belief that there is no absolute truth. Satan used Scripture to challenge Jesus' identity, but it was a perverted reinterpretation of Scripture rather than its true meaning. If, as a postmodern world view states, there is no absolute truth, Satan's reinterpretation of the Scripture is both possible and plausible, and his strategy becomes tremendously effective and powerful. However, Jesus responded with absolute truth.

Postmodernism proposes that truth and morality are relative, meaning judging what is good or bad, right or wrong, or truth or lie should only be assessed relative to a particular, limited point of view. Stated simply, postmodern thought claims the truth is whatever the individual decides it is. Only fact is seen as objective, while judgments of truth are seen as subjective. In this philosophy of thought, reality is based on individual perception, and everything is seen in reference to the self. It brings to mind II Timothy 3:2-7 (excerpts): "People will be lovers of themselves… boastful, proud…unholy…not lovers of the good…conceited… swayed by all kinds of evil desires, always learning but never able to come to a knowledge of the truth." A common postmodern statement would be, "Well, that is *your* truth," indicating that truth varies from person to person based on perception, belief, and context. You may be familiar with another postmodern response: "It depends on what the meaning of the word *is* is."

The problem inherent in postmodern thought as it relates to identity is, if there is no absolute truth, you can never truly know who you are. According to postmodernism, your identity changes based on context and perception, leaving you constantly questioning and open to the whims of opinion. Your self-image can be crushed with one critical word or shaken by one difficult circumstance. In addition, postmodern thought challenges the certainty of the truth of Scripture, so you are left with nothing to use as an anchor for your understanding of yourself as God's creation. The absence of any absolute truth leaves you without a secure foundation, giving external conditions and feedback tremendous power over how you feel about yourself. Any wind of circumstance can knock your view of yourself awry.

In his third temptation, Satan attempted to shift Jesus' focus from His identity to external factors. Jesus responded by centering Himself on God and truth. However, what if truth was relative? What if all you could know about yourself were the facts of your life at the moment? Your identity would be chained to whatever could be proven about your situation for that day. In this postmodern world, people often introduce themselves by sharing what they do, or if they are married or single and if they have children, as if that tells the other person who they are. This very typical response indicates the tendency to equate identity with external factors. However, any belief that identity is based on external factors is very damaging to how you view yourself. For example, if your spouse cheats on you, you can start to believe you have no value, if you have relied on being married to determine your identity. If you are fired from your job, you can feel a profound loss of worth, if your identity has been wrapped up in your work, and you've felt your value was based on what you produced.

All external factors, including position, possessions, role, status, wealth, and appearance are transient and temporary. When you rely on anything other than your internal design to define you, you are continually anxious, because on some level you know those external things can be gone or changed in an instant, leaving you with a profound sense of uncertainty and a vacuum in your understanding of yourself. As a result, your identity, as you understand it, is constantly under threat. In addition, you will always have some level of fear if you rely on input from others (i.e., friends, spouse, parents, societal opinions of what is approved, etc.) to feel acceptable and valued. Do you find yourself making decisions based on fear (meaning your choices are often directed by some attempt to control or avoid pain)? If so, *you are allowing external things to provide, bolster, or influence your understanding of who you are.* This plays right into the enemy's hands and is not in alignment with God's desire or plan.

TRUE IDENTITY

Your true identity is based on how God says He created you and who He made you to be. Scripture tells us we are made by Him,

31

and His life is the light within us (John 1:3-4). He "made His light shine in our hearts" (II Corinthians 4:6). In other words, God's nature expressed in His creation of you is your identity. Contemplate that statement. Meditate on it for a few minutes. You have God's light within your being. God expresses Himself through your identity. The profound honor God has for you, demonstrated in these truths, is almost beyond expression. Therefore, your identity is most precious and needs to be valued and protected. If you love and value God, you, by definition, love and value yourself. Do you recognize and treat with honor the great treasure of your identity?

Instead of floating through life, unanchored, when you begin to recognize what God "knit together" to create your true identity (which contains the expression of God within you), this revelation of who you are starts to build a "floor" beneath your feet. One stone at a time, He grounds you and gives you stable footing. Where you were rooted in lies, He anchors you in secure and certain truth. The "shifting sand" becomes a rock that cannot be moved. From this sure footing, you can allow your identity to flow freely from your heart into the world, and the outflow of your identity fulfills your purpose. When you live from your true heart, your life reflects God (Proverbs 27:19).

Because your true identity is unchangeable and secure, knowing your identity is like a shield which deflects "all the flaming arrows of the evil one" (Ephesians 6:16) and provides you an unshakable foundation from which to live. The sphere in which you live in unity with Jesus, without any external measurement of your worth, becomes your protection. His peace becomes your peace; His joy becomes your joy. The enemy is powerless against you, because if he can't deceive you about your identity, all of his other deceptions begin to fall apart, revealed as the smoke and mirrors they actually are by the truth of God within you.

Thus, your identity is your most powerful weapon in spiritual warfare. Doesn't this make sense? You've seen how Satan's temptations were focused on challenging Jesus' identity, which suggests identity is the largest threat to the enemy's goals. It stands to reason, then, when you are certain of who you are, as Jesus was when tempted by the enemy, you will stand as He stood, in assurance and strength. When you stand on the truths of who you are as your foundation, nothing else – no action of another person toward you, no word spoken against you, no other belief about you – has power over you. You can stand firm and without fear because you know only God determines who you are, and nothing can undermine what God says about you. God, as your Creator, is the only author of your identity. God is enough; therefore, you are enough.

When your life is an outflow of your true identity, your circumstances no longer determine how you feel, how you see yourself, or how you view the world (Philippians 4:11; I Thessalonians 5:18). Remember how the lies of the enemy, through seeds planted in childhood and nurtured by him through your circumstances, become a "lens" through which you interpret all of life? If the truth of your identity, revealed by Jesus in your heart, becomes your foundation, those lies are blown away like so much dust scattered by the wind. Instead of lies, your "lens" through which you see all things is the lens of who you are in Christ. When bad things happen, which they will, you always have the sure foundation of who you are to return to. Like Jesus in the wilderness, you have a rebuttal to the enemy's temptations. If you lose your job, instead of responding, "I'm worthless" or "I'm not good enough," you respond, "I know who I am, and I know I'm valuable." If your spouse leaves you, instead of saying, "I'm unloved" or "I don't matter," you are able to say with certainty, "I know I'm truly and deeply loved for who I am." No matter how terrible the events, your certainty can't be moved. This is the definition of faith: being certain of things hoped for and having the knowledge of things unseen (Hebrews 11:1).

God meant you to be exactly and precisely who you are, with the aspects of His nature He chose to knit into you. His desire is for you to embrace this nature completely, including the downsides of it. Wait…there are downsides? Absolutely. Because you have been given aspects of His nature but are not God and do not have His full nature, you have "missing pieces," so to speak. Those missing elements are the downsides of being you. You are perfectly imperfect. Just as God planned, the elements of His nature you don't have are aspects you rely on Him to provide for you through your relationship with Him and His presence in your heart. For example, my foundational nature reflects Jesus on the steps of the Temple confronting the Pharisees or turning over the tables of the moneychangers. However, this identity doesn't include Jesus' patience and mercy, so I rely on Jesus to provide these qualities for me through the presence of His Spirit within me. When my clients or students say to me, "You're so patient," I always respond, "You can literally thank God."

He wants you to embrace all aspects of your nature, including the downsides, because He loves you just as you are, including the missing pieces. When you acknowledge both the wonder of your identity, and its downsides, you are able to allow the beauty of you to express freely while turning to Jesus to provide everything lacking, so the full and true expression of yourself is what flows out into the world.

CONCLUSION

By His will and choice, you have your nature (Revelation 4:11) and "participate in the divine nature" (II Peter 1:4). God sees you – and not from a distance, looking down on you – not in a general way, like one of a vast number. He sees you with an extremely personal and specific knowledge of who you are, inside and out, thoroughly and completely seen and known. Beyond seeing and knowing you, He accepts you and loves you *exactly and precisely* for who you are. He will never treat you as less than or any differently from who He sees and knows you to be, even when you aren't living out your true identity and are acting instead based on the impositions of the sin nature and the enemy's lies. He will never settle for less than you fully being who He created. This is the *loving goodness* of God.

You are the light of God. Reflected in you is some aspect of God's nature, meant to shine brightly into this dark world to bring His light and overcome the darkness. The enemy would have you smother that light and hide it – don't agree to hide it. He would claim you aren't worthy of being out on a stand, that you would be safer hidden in a clay jar or put beneath a bed (Luke 8:16), that no one cares to see your unique light; or, that you don't shine at all. Don't listen. Let your light shine before others (Matthew 5:16) by allowing the nature God placed in you to flow freely from your heart so that all will see His face in you. Refuse to hide anymore.

Your true nature is all He desires, and that nature is enough. He has made room for you to be you. As Jesus said, "My Father's house has many rooms" (John 14:2). The truth of this kind of love sets you free (John 8:32):

Free to express who you are, no matter how others respond to it or what others say about it, because you already know how He responds and what He says;

Free to accept both the good sides and the downsides of your nature because He accepts them and loves them;

Free to just be, without striving, because His love is freely lavished on you and cannot be earned;

Free to stop judging yourself, so that by extension you stop judging others;

Free to leave shame behind, because you are wholly and utterly seen, known, and loved.

Free from fear, having a solid foundation, unshakable and immovable, that no circumstance can alter.

Peace comes from resting in who you are, knowing that He is within you and infuses every part of your being with His deep love. Joy comes from the expression of your true nature flowing freely into the world, unhindered and unencumbered. The precious treasure of your identity is the cornerstone piece of the map on your quest for the Kingdom life.

STARTING POINT: QUESTIONS TO EXPLORE IDENTITY

Answer the following questions to further explore your identity in Christ. Consider your answers prayerfully and thoughtfully. Don't offer a superficial response and move on to the next question but look deeply within and be as honest with yourself as you can be. Avoid giving "pat" answers you might have heard in church, particularly if you've not examined what those responses mean in depth. These questions are designed to help you understand what you believe now about who you are, and to begin to explore what God wants to say to you about your identity.

1. How would you describe your identity?
2. What characteristics of Jesus' nature do you see expressed in your identity? (Use the list offered in the section of your Map Key titled "The Example of Jesus" as a starting point.)
3. How has the enemy tempted you to doubt your identity?
4. What seeds of lies about your identity were planted in your childhood?
5. What circumstances or events in your life have reinforced and deepened the roots of those lies?
6. In what ways have you equated your identity with external factors?
7. When are you most likely to make decisions based on fear?
8. What downsides do you see to your identity? (Look again at elements of Jesus' nature to recognize "missing pieces" from your identity.)
9. In what ways have you settled for being less than who God created you to be?
10. What judgments have you made about yourself? What judgments have you made about others?

DESTINATION: PRAYERS TO UNCOVER IDENTITY

Find a quiet place with few distractions to sit with Jesus. Still your mind and quiet your heart by repeating a verse of Scripture meaningful to you; for example, you could repeat, "You have searched me, oh Lord, and you know me" (Psalm 139:1). I have written a prayer for you as an example, but use your own words, from your heart, to ask Jesus to reveal your identity to you: *Lord, You created me and You know me better than anyone. I seek to know myself through Your eyes. Would you please show me how you see me? Would you tell me who You created me to be?*

After you pray, spend time in silent meditation, eyes closed and listening for His answers. He may show you an image in your mind, a symbolic representation of your identity. He may bring to your mind certain words or phrases, such as "servant's heart" or "shining light." He might bring to mind a particular verse or story from Scripture that reveals some aspect of your nature. You can recognize responses from the Lord by the peace they stir up in your heart. If an image or word comes to you that brings anxiety or shame, reject it, recenter yourself on Jesus, and ask again. Otherwise, don't analyze what comes up or question if it's the Lord. Instead, go with it and follow wherever He takes you. If you are getting "off base," He will let you know. Keep with it, asking Jesus to explain anything you don't understand and to show you more, until you feel He is finished.

If you don't hear anything, don't be concerned or frustrated. Remember, we have an enemy who actively opposes our treasure seeking and tries to thwart our connection with Jesus. Take a break and come back to your prayer later. This time, if you don't receive a response, ask Jesus what is in the way. It may be a lie you believe about yourself, such as you are unworthy or shameful, or it may be distractions of life he is using to get in your way. False beliefs about God can also hinder making a connection; for example, fearing God is ashamed of you or is punishing you for something you've done in the past can cause distance in your relationship with Him. Whatever Jesus reveals is in the way, ask Him to bring truth to your heart to move the hindrance out of your way. Then return to your prayer request.

Another prayer request you could make is to ask Jesus to tell you what your Kingdom name is. Here is an example of a prayer asking for your spiritual name: *Lord, Your word tells me You have a white stone for me, on which is written my new name, known only to You and me (Revelation 2:17). I seek my new name, the one You gave me. Would You please show me the white stone that has my name written on it? Would You explain the meaning of my new name and tell me what it reveals about my identity?*

Once again, after you pray, spend time listening quietly and follow up with further exploration of anything you receive. When Jesus gave me my Kingdom name, Helga, He showed me an image of a Viking warrior, sword drawn, overlooking enemy ships approaching from the sea. Then, as I asked Him about the vision, He gave me another picture, this time of the dance scene between Anna and the King in *The King and I.* So, I understood my full Kingdom name is Helga Anna, the spiritual warrior who is also a free-spirit lover of the King. He may show you an image, like He did for me, or He may simply tell you the name He gave you. Continue to explore what He shares with you, asking Him for more explanation and greater understanding, until you feel at peace that you have received your new name in your heart.

Another approach is to identify one aspect of your nature you are certain is true of you, one you already know. Take that piece of the puzzle to Jesus in prayer and ask Him to reveal what else you can know about your nature from knowing that one aspect. This prayer might be something like: *Lord, I know You created me with a compassionate heart (fill in with whatever you are sure is true of you). Would You show me what else is true of someone who has a compassionate heart like Yours? Are those things also true of me? What do those qualities tell me about my identity?* In this example, He might show you how someone with a compassionate heart is also kind, sensitive, empathic, loving, and giving. Then, as you allow Him to build your "floor" with these individual stones, ask Him to show you what they create as a whole.

A great way to turn the enemy's tactics against him is to examine his attacks against you to see what he is trying to accomplish. When you see what he is attempting to destroy, you will see an aspect of your nature revealed. This type of prayer would be along these lines: *Lord, the enemy is constantly trying to tell me I am weak and powerless (fill in with whatever the enemy is using against you or trying to cover up in you). That must mean You have made me strong. Would You tell me more about the strength and power You have given me? What other qualities go along with that strength?* In this case, the enemy fears your strength, so he is trying to make you believe it isn't true; in fact, he is saying the opposite is true. He often uses an opposite characteristic to attack your true nature, but you can turn the tables on him using this kind of prayer.

Finally, a great way to uncover your identity is to consider which Scriptural story or stories about Jesus touch your heart the most and what qualities Jesus exhibits in those stories. You can then make that story the focal point of your prayer. An example of this type of prayer is: *Lord, I am drawn to Your <u>loving kindness with the woman at the well</u> (fill in with the quality or qualities of Jesus from the story you chose). Did You give me those same qualities when You created me? What do those qualities tell me about my identity? In what ways am I like You in this story?* If you are drawn to a story, you already relate to it in some way. When Jesus reveals the deeper connection between the story and your identity, you will appreciate the story even more. You can also explore in prayer other Scripture stories that demonstrate those same qualities and see what you can learn about yourself through them.

Any or all of these prayers are effective to bring you to Jesus with openness in your heart, a willingness to seek your treasure, and a focal point to help you look and listen for His responses.

Uncovering your identity is a process. Jesus will continue to build upon what you receive through these prayers, expanding your insight and deepening your understanding, as He reveals to you how your unique, special identity brings His presence into the world.

SETTING THE COURSE: LIVING YOUR IDENTITY

The first section presents concepts you may want to internalize, and the second section lists some actions you may take to apply the information you have studied. Approach the following concepts and actions prayerfully. Avoid any thinking that you must rigidly adhere to them, because these are only suggestions and may not work for you. Everyone is different. Remember, you are one-of-a-kind. Use these suggestions to begin to build your own repertoire of tools and weapons you can use on your quest to live the Kingdom life.

INTERNALIZE THE CONCEPTS

Consider the wonder of your own creation. Meditate on the amount of intricate detail and unfettered love that went into making you. Think about the details of your DNA, your cells and body structures, your mind and consciousness, your emotions, and your identity. Contemplate what it means that God would desire to express His nature into your being.

Consider the times in your life you feel most at peace. Examine if those times are instances when you are "being" rather than focusing on "doing." Contemplate how you could "be" in life instead of simply doing what you believe is expected or required.

Consider what you love the most about Jesus. Observe your relationships with those you love and see what qualities you see expressed by you in those relationships. Examine any intersections between what you love about Jesus and how you love others.

Consider ways in which you have allowed your past experiences to define you instead of accepting how Jesus sees you as your identity. Meditate on these truths in concert: circumstances cannot define you; God alone, as your Creator, decided who you would be; God's nature expressed in His creation of you is your identity.

Consider your imperfections. Visualize Jesus embracing those imperfections with love. See Him filling you with anything you need or lack. Contemplate the meaning of the phrase, "perfectly imperfect."

Imagine a floor beneath your feet made of individual stones, each stone bearing an inscription with one of your qualities. See any empty spaces beyond the stones, ones that are yet to be filled in to complete the floor. Visualize yourself standing solidly on the completed stones, certain and confident and at peace. Picture Jesus placing stones in the empty spaces and read what those stones say.

PROCESS THEIR APPLICATION

Begin each day recalling your identity and expressing gratitude to God for His creation of you and His love expressed to you through His nature as a part of your identity (I Thessalonians 5:18). Prayerfully ask Jesus to help you live from your true heart throughout the day.

Notice areas of your life where your true identity has not been welcomed or accepted. Begin to set boundaries regarding how you will be expressing your true nature in the future. Begin eliminating from your life any aspects of it where your boundaries are not accepted. Keep in mind, no one can change who God created you to be or make you stop being you, so I'm not referring to isolating yourself or avoiding circumstances that may be difficult. I am talking specifically about optional activities or negative relationships that attempt to demand of you to be someone other than your true self.

Throughout each day, focus on the here and now (Matthew 6:34). If you find your thoughts wandering to the past, gently reorient them to the present by noticing your surroundings, taking a few deep breaths, and checking in with Jesus in prayer (just a brief,

"What would You like to focus on now?" and listening for a response is enough).

Begin adding to your life people who see who you are and encourage you to express your true identity. Add to your life new ways you can allow your true identity to flow out into others and into the world (I Thessalonians 5:11).

Pray continually throughout the day (I Thessalonians 5:17). You don't have to go into a private place to pray; you can do a quick check-in, like "How are we doing?" or, "Is there anything you want to say to me?" and listen briefly for His response wherever you are, no matter what you're doing.

If your peace is disrupted, stop what you are doing and pray, asking Jesus to show you what lie belief the enemy is trying to stir in you, then ask for His revelation of the truth. Allow the truth He brings to push the lie away from you. Then, recenter in prayer on your true identity and ask Jesus to heal any wounds the enemy caused through the lie belief (Philippians 4:6-7).

End each day with a celebration of who you are. Offer praise and thanksgiving to Jesus for His help and partnership with you throughout the day (I Peter 2:9).

TWO

The Treasure of Authority

YOUR COMPASS

*In my vision at night I looked, and there before me was one like a
son of man, coming with the clouds of heaven. He approached the
Ancient of Days and was led into his presence. He was given
authority, glory and sovereign power; all nations and peoples of
every language worshiped him. His dominion is an everlasting
dominion that will not pass away, and his kingdom is one that will
never be destroyed. Then the sovereignty, power and greatness of
all the kingdoms under heaven will be handed over to the holy
people of the Most High (Daniel 7:13-15, 27).*

*He raised Christ from the dead and seated him at his right hand in
the heavenly realms, far above all rule and authority, power and
dominion, and every name that is invoked, not only in the present
age but also in the one to come. And God placed all things under his
feet and appointed him to be head over everything for the*

45

*church, which is his body, the fullness of him who fills everything in
every way (Ephesians 1:20-23).*

*I have given you authority to trample on snakes and scorpions and
to overcome all the power of the enemy (Luke 10:19.)*

*For the Spirit God gave us does not make us timid, but gives us
power, love and self-discipline (II Timothy 1:7).*

*This day I call the heavens and the earth as witnesses against you
that I have set before you life and death, blessings and curses. Now
choose life, so that you and your children may live and that you may
love the LORD your God, listen to his voice, and hold fast to him.
For the LORD is your life (Deuteronomy 30:19-20).*

*"I have the right to do anything," you say—but not everything is
beneficial. "I have the right to do anything"—but not everything is
constructive (I Corinthians 10:23).*

*Each one should test their own actions. Do not be deceived: God
cannot be mocked. A man reaps what he sows. Whoever sows to
please their flesh, from the flesh will reap destruction; whoever
sows to please the Spirit, from the Spirit will reap eternal
life (Galatians 6:4, 7-8).*

*Multitudes, multitudes in the valley of decision! For the day of
the LORD is near in the valley of decision (Joel 3:14).*

As Jesus and his disciples were on their way, he came to a village where a woman named Martha opened her home to him. She had a sister called Mary, who sat at the Lord's feet listening to what he said. But Martha was distracted by all the preparations that had to be made. She came to him and asked, "Lord, don't you care that my sister has left me to do the work by myself? Tell her to help me!" "Martha, Martha," the Lord answered, "you are worried and upset about many things, but few things are needed—or indeed only one. Mary has chosen what is better, and it will not be taken away from her" (Luke 10:38-42).

MAP KEY: AGENCY, OWNERSHIP, AND CHOICE

AUTHORITY DEFINED

*Y*ou have been given His authority.

Authority as a treasure is often overlooked or minimized in its importance, but it is such a crucial element of the Kingdom, it is matched in importance by identity only. In fact, identity and authority are so inextricably intertwined, to express your true nature fully, you must also employ your God-given authority.

So, what is authority? Authority is best defined as the right to make decisions and direct someone or something. Inherent in understanding authority is the concept of choice, which is the act of making a decision between two or more possibilities. Your God-given authority is what gives you the right to choose; in other words, free will.

Authority has everything to do with choice but nothing to do with control, which is a very important distinction. Control assumes outcomes are or can be determined, but, in truth, you cannot determine outcomes. Many variables and other factors come into play alongside your choices; for example, the exercise of free will in others impacts what happens as a result of your choices. For example, I can choose to leave for work in plenty of time to arrive by 8 am, but someone else choosing to speed and causing an accident in front of me, followed by lightning striking a tree which falls across the road, will still make me late. You make your choices, and whatever flows from your choices interacts with the choices of others and the circumstances in which the choices are made.

In fact, control is an illusion, another lie of the enemy. When you try to control (determine outcomes), you are left feeling powerless, since outcomes cannot be determined. As such, a belief in control hinders the actual exercise of authority through choice. The exercise of authority brings freedom. Attempts to control only result in anxiety and fear. When you try to control, you become a puppet of the person or thing you are trying to control. This is the paradox of the kingdom of God. It is only through our freedom of choice that we are truly empowered.

God is sovereign, which means all authority belongs to Him. Scripture states God is sovereign 297 times. Do you know how many times Scripture says, "God is in control"? Zero. Unlike control, often wrongly ascribed to God, sovereignty is related to authority. Just as authority is the *right* to make decisions, sovereignty is the *right* to rule. God, since He is sovereign, has the *right* to set the design and function of His created system, to establish the order of things, and to write the law; however, sovereignty does not include determining outcomes, which control assumes. An earthly king, for example, establishes the rule of law and order but doesn't determine who will follow the law and who disobeys it.

Because control prevents the freedom to choose, in His authority, God chooses not to control. Instead, He chooses to share His authority with you. He designed you with the same ability and freedom to choose as He has (remember, you are made in His image). Consider the depth of love God has for you that He would give you such a precious gift, the gift of sharing in His authority, knowing it could mean you might reject Him.

From the beginning, God extended His authority to humankind. In addition to the right to make their own choices, the first created human beings were given authority over the other creatures on the earth and were allowed to name them (Genesis 1:26, 2:19). His will, the decision to give authority and choice to humans, was the act that set everything else in the rest of the Scriptural story in motion.

Without having a choice, you would not be capable of love, since love, to be considered love, must be freely given. Your relationship with God would not be possible without your right to choose. You wouldn't be able to offer or receive love at all if you had no free will, because love is impossible in the absence of freedom to choose. If God was going to create you to reflect His image, to receive His love, and to be in relationship with Him, He also had to give you authority, the right to choose. Since the whole of Scripture is the story of God's loving pursuit of His children, there would be no story without God's extension of authority to His creation.

Without having a choice, Eve could not have been tempted by the serpent, and Adam could not have chosen to take the fruit from Eve and eat it; in fact, without choice, the knowledge of good and evil could not exist. So, the tree of the knowledge of good and evil was in the garden with Adam and Eve *because* they were given authority. Therefore, God's decision to extend His authority to humankind was a decision to go to the cross, and our having authority was that important to Him – He was willing to die for it.

Because of the vast, boundless, and gracious love of God, you have the authority to choose to follow Jesus or to reject Him. Jesus called to each disciple with a simple, "Come, follow me" (Matthew 4:19, Luke 5:27, John 1:43), and they could have chosen to remain doing exactly what they were doing when He called them, but that's not what they chose. They left their nets, put down their duties, and left everything behind to follow Jesus. By contrast, the rich young ruler chose to walk away, because he didn't want to lose his worldly wealth (Matthew 19:21-22). So, salvation and redemption also depend on choice.

Do you see how vitally important authority is in the Kingdom? Authority is the fulcrum on which everything else rests; it is the pivotal element in your life. God's very nature depends on authority (since He is love – I John 4:8), which means your nature depends on it, too. Choice empowers your freedom, the expression of your identity, your ability to give and receive love, your deliverance from death, your purpose, and your relationship with God. Without choice, you are left with emptiness, futility,

50

powerlessness, hopelessness, and death. Simply stated, everything rides on the treasure of authority.

AGENCY AND OWNERSHIP

God has given you authority over yourself; your body, your thoughts, your emotions, your choices, your actions, your responses, your feelings – all are yours to decide and direct. This personal authority is called agency, which is the individual capacity to act independently and make your own free choices.

No one else has authority over you. No one can "make" you feel or believe something against your will. If someone tries to impose their will onto you, attempting to impede your agency through intimidation or other expressions of power or control (for example, through abuse or threats), you retain your authority over how you will respond and what you will feel and believe. In other words, you always have a choice, no matter what your circumstances.

Likewise, you do not have authority over anyone else's choices. Just like you, others have agency. You cannot "make" others feel or believe anything. Within the space marked by the outer edges of your body, you retain authority, but that authority doesn't extend beyond that space. God's desire and will is for you to have agency, but not control – not over your circumstances, and not over others. This same desire and will applies to everyone. Just as others cannot take away your choice, you don't have the power or authority to remove the choices of others.

Blurring the boundary lines between what is yours and what belongs to someone else causes great difficulty in relationships and undermines personal peace and contentment. Have you heard the

51

saying, "Good fences make good neighbors"? This same adage applies to personal boundaries. Remember, your feelings and beliefs and choices are yours, and yours alone. Don't step over the "fence" of your neighbor and start pulling weeds in their garden, including taking ownership of how they feel or what they believe or choose to do. At the same time, when others attempt to bulldoze past your "fence," reestablish your boundary line and choose your own feelings, beliefs, and actions.

How do you know if you are mistakenly taking ownership of what, in truth, belongs to others? When you hear yourself saying or thinking you "made" someone feel a certain way, or that someone else "made" you feel how you're feeling, stop and reevaluate. The truth is you don't have the authority to determine someone else's feelings, and others always have the choice over what they are going to feel. In the same way, no one can "make" you feel anything. Your feelings and beliefs occur within the boundary of your agency, inside the dividing line created by your physical body, so they are yours to choose. Believing anything else leaves you with the illusion others have power over you and undermines living in your God-ordained agency.

Boundary blurring is particularly evident when problems occur in relationships. You may discover during disagreements with others is when you struggle the most with boundary confusion. I suggest two very useful questions to ask yourself whenever difficulties arise: 1) Is this a weed in my garden? 2) Who owns this problem? Anything that is not your choice to make is not a weed in your garden, and anything that you don't get to choose is not your problem to own. So, if someone you care about is upset with you based on a choice they made, but they didn't ask you for input on

52

the decision, the answer to question one is "no." If they ask for input and you offer it, but they continue to make bad choices, the answer to question one remains "no." Since they are the ones choosing, the answer to question two, in both cases, is "they own this problem." Knowing these truths, you can then return to a place of peace, understanding the choice is beyond your authority and their anger is falsely directed.

CHOICE AND RESPONSIBILITY

You only have ownership over problems caused by choices you make (Galatians 6:4, 7-8). While it is very important you don't take ownership over someone else's problems, it is equally important you own the consequences created by your choices. This is called taking responsibility.

It can be painful to accept responsibility for your choices. As discussed in the last chapter, the enemy likes to tempt you with ways to take care of yourself and provide for your own needs, such as avoiding anything painful or difficult, so you may be enticed to divert blame onto others instead of accepting responsibility for things you have chosen and the consequences of those choices. Satan wants to set you up to blame others for your feelings and choices, as in, "they made me feel _____" or "I did it because they did _____" or "if they would just _____, then I would be ok" or "it's their fault I _____."

However, when he offers the temptation, Satan fails to let you in on the secret that loss of agency, with the resultant loss of freedom, is much more painful than the temporary sting of admitting your choice was wrong. Failure to take responsibility for your choices leads to an interruption in agency, because it assumes the person or circumstance you are blaming has power over your choice. You are left feeling like a powerless victim instead of a free individual with agency.

From the other end of the spectrum, the enemy also wants you to accept responsibility for others, agreeing that what they are doing or feeling is your fault, or you are responsible for how others act because of how you 'made' them feel. You are then enticed to try to 'fix' things for them instead of allowing them to accept their own responsibility. Your thought is, "if I would just _____, then the other person would feel better or would be happy." In agreeing with this lie, you enable others to remain victims and interrupt their possibility of growth and change. In addition, you are left with a profound sense of shame, but you are powerless to do anything to make it better because it isn't your choice to make.

In truth, you cannot be responsible for how others feel or what they choose, because God has given others agency and has given you authority over one thing and one thing only: yourself. He is clear that over yourself, you have been given full authority, and Christ has provided you with true freedom in all ways (Galatians 5:1; II Corinthians 3:17; Ephesians 3:12). Living in the truth of your choice and responsibility brings great freedom. Taking responsibility for your choices and refusing responsibility for the choices of others protects your authority and prevents others, including the enemy, from usurping it.

Taking responsibility also involves change, in the form of making different choices. The word "repent" means to turn away from and dedicate yourself to change. Jesus calls you to repentance, but not to satisfy some arbitrary rule to earn forgiveness. Repentance is there for your benefit. When you recognize a choice was wrong, take responsibility for your choice, and make a different choice next time, your freedom is restored, and your life is improved, all without shame and condemnation. In truth, one of the wonderful things about authority is that you *always* can make a different choice. If you don't like one choice you've made, simply choose again and choose differently. What freedom Jesus has provided for you!

Jesus said, "I have given you authority to trample on snakes and scorpions and to overcome all the power of the enemy" (Luke 10:19). Can you see why Satan tries to usurp your personal authority, impede your agency, and limit your choices? He benefits directly if you believe you are a victim, powerless in your circumstances, so you won't use the authority Jesus gave you to overcome Satan's power. It furthers his agenda if you enable others and expend your energy and effort toward a futile pursuit of "making" someone else happy instead of standing against the enemy's schemes.

However, Satan cannot "make" you believe him or agree with him. Such is the power of authority. If you refuse to agree with the enemy's lies, he is powerless to do anything. By giving you authority, God made it possible for the enemy to be defeated. This truth is both surprising and relieving; surprising in that God giving you authority creates the enemy's defeat and relieving in that he has so little real power, a choice is all it takes to defeat him.

If you were God, you might be tempted to exert control over your creation, trying to prevent a bad outcome. Think about how parents often try to control their children and the frequent result of such attempts to control. Children who are controlled often rebel, and when they don't rebel, they acquiesce, living in fear instead of living in the fullness of who God created them to be. Either way, the child is wounded by the control. So, in trying to prevent a bad outcome, the parent creates a bad outcome. Control works that way, producing the opposite of what was intended. What the parent meant as loving in trying to control outcomes to prevent pain was actually damaging.

God is a perfect Father, loving in all His choices. Rather than sentencing his children to a forever torment by the enemy, He gave us choice. As a result, we can *choose* to reject the enemy's deceptions, leaving him powerless over us. Only God could've created such an upside-down way to defeat Satan!

Of course, because you have choice, you can also choose to believe the enemy's lies. The warnings in Galatians 5:13 (You, my brothers and sisters, were called to be free. But do not use your freedom to indulge the flesh; rather, serve one another humbly in love), I Peter 2:16 (Live as free people, but do not use your freedom as a cover-up for evil), and Galatians 6:4, 7-8 (Each one should test their own actions. Do not be deceived: God cannot be mocked. A man reaps what he sows. Whoever sows to please their flesh, from the flesh will reap destruction; whoever sows to please the Spirit, from the Spirit will reap eternal life) speak to the importance of choosing wisely in your freedom.

MAKING CHOICES

Knowing you have agency through the authority given to you by God, and knowing you are responsible for how you express your authority in your choices, how then do you know how to choose well? What are the choices that lead to a Kingdom life?

Scripture shares a story of two contrasting choices. Jesus and His disciples were visiting in the home of Mary, Martha, and Lazarus. Martha was distracted, felt mistreated, and was perhaps disappointed in what she saw as a lack of intervention by the Lord. Mary, on the other hand, sat at Jesus' feet, listening to every word He said. When questioned by Martha, who was caught up in preparations and upset with her sister, Mary, the Lord responded, "you are worried and upset about many things, but few things are needed—or indeed only one. Mary has chosen what is better, and it will not be taken away from her." (Luke 10:41-42).

This story presents the difference between choosing the ways of the world (Ephesians 2:1-3; I Corinthians 3:1-3) vs. choosing to fix your eyes on Jesus (II Corinthians 4:18; Hebrews 12:2). According to Jesus, only one thing is needed: Him. Do you choose to sit at Jesus' feet and listen to every word He says, like Mary? Do you partner with Jesus in making choices, or do you react to the demands of the world, like Martha? Do you choose to focus on His presence with you through each and every moment in your life, or are you focused on the experiences and circumstances themselves? Like Martha, you may be easily caught up in the distractions thrown at you by the enemy and all the things you buy into as "have to's" that you lose sight of what is truly important. When it all comes down to the bottom line, Jesus is more important than anything else in your life. He is your one true need.

So, what truths can you learn from the story of Martha and Mary? I have listed four truths for your consideration:

1. Worry does nothing for you

You can get tricked into thinking worry will prevent something bad from happening or will prepare you adequately for whatever is coming. You might buy Satan's lie that fear is a good shield for you. You may fall into self-protection mode very easily but worry and fear don't protect you. In fact, fear is the sister of control, and like control, produces the opposite from your intended result. You always create what you most fear.

2. Being with Jesus is the better choice.

In place of worry and self-protection, Jesus offers you His presence. "So what?" you may be saying. "What good is Him being there to me? I still have to go through whatever is happening." The question reveals what is missing: an awareness of what His presence brings. He brings peace even during suffering, peace which guards your hearts and minds (Philippians 4:7), and He brings truth that sets you free (John 8:32).

3. There are no "have to's."

I've heard many people say in response to this story that Martha was right, the meal still "had to" be made, the home still "had to" be prepared. My response is, "Did it?" Would Jesus have been upset or disappointed if Martha had sat beside Him listening to every word He said, like Mary was doing? This story says no, He would not. Was the meal the most important thing? Jesus is clearly saying He wanted Martha to choose what is better. Perhaps Martha could've waited until Jesus was finished teaching truth, and then invited Him to come with her to prepare the meal together. I firmly believe He would've been happy to come and would've served them all gladly. How often do you see things as a "have to" and miss opportunities to be with the Lord?

4. You can always listen to Jesus.

No matter what your circumstances may be, the Lord is always present with you and is always willing to show you truth. You may not always know that you are hearing the voice of the Lord, due to interferences like Martha experienced, and you may feel at times that He is far away, but Scripture tells us He never leaves you (Deuteronomy 31:3, Hebrews 13:5). When other things are in the way of your comprehending or hearing His voice, you can rest in the truth that listening to Him, as Mary did, is something He has said will not be taken away. This truth encourages you to be persistent, and to ask Him what is in your way instead of wondering where He is.

Another story of choice occurs in II Samuel 24, after David had sinned against God. David was offered three choices to serve as the consequence of his actions (verses 12-13); two of the choices would come against the land and the people, and one would affect David only. David begged God not to give him the consequence of falling into human hands (verse 14), so a plague fell on the land. When David saw his people dying, he realized what he had done and was greatly distressed (verse 17), saying he was their shepherd; yet, he allowed his sheep to suffer in his place. So, David begged

God to withdraw the plague and give the consequence to him. This story is an example of choosing for self over choosing for love.

The greatest example of a choice made for love was made by Jesus in Gethsemane (Mark 14:35-36). Jesus was troubled in His soul and distressed, knowing what He was facing the following day. Yet, His choice was to say, "not what I will but what You will." At that moment, He could've chosen to walk away. He could've chosen for self. What an astounding choice, knowing what He faced! Instead, He chose for love, and our reclamation is the result.

What truths can you gain from these contrasting stories of David and Jesus? I would like to suggest a few takeaways for you:

1. Don't listen to fear.

    Like control, fear produces the opposite result from what you desire. David thought he was choosing what benefitted him the most; yet, what he found was the consequence of his choice was unbearable. Choosing based on fear doesn't produce happiness or satisfaction or safety. Fear sends you 180 degrees from where God is moving, so listening to fear ultimately leads to your destruction (I John 4:18).

2. Selfish choices produce pain for both you and others.

    David thought he was sparing himself pain when he chose the consequence to fall on others instead of himself, but what he experienced was the deeper pain of facing what he had done. Contrast his distress with

Jesus, who, once He made His choice for love, walked forward in perfect peace. If you sow for self, you reap destruction. This has been true since Adam and Eve. "Do nothing out of selfish ambition or vain conceit. Rather, in humility value others above yourselves" (Philippians 2:3).

3. Love is the greatest choice.

    Jesus commanded you to love as He loves you (John 15:12, 17). When asked to name the greatest commandment, Jesus answered love (Mark 12:30-31). Jesus took the commandment to love your neighbor as yourself even farther and turned upside down what it means to love when He taught His disciples to love their enemies (Matthew 5:43-47). In every way, Jesus demonstrated love is the greatest choice you can make.

4. Choosing based on love produces good fruit in you and others.

    No one would question the fruit of Jesus' choice. His suffering and death ransomed all people from the wages of sin, provided a way to truly know God in a real and personal way, and sent the ripple effects of love across the world. While it is true some great evils have been done in Jesus' name, none of those evils were in alignment with God's will or Christ's teachings; instead, most of them were perpetrated out of fear or for power and control, and Paul warned of the consequences of choices made without love (I Corinthians 13:1-3). But the positive and miraculous transformations in individual's lives and in the world because of the *love* of Jesus cannot be denied. "The greatest of these is love" (I Corinthians 13:13).

So, based on these Scriptural truths, how do you make choices? Instead of worry, Jesus offers peace. Walk in the direction of peace and allow His peace to guard your heart and mind in Him. Instead of self-protection, Jesus offers His shield of truth. Seek truth before making a choice and allow His truth to provide protection against the enemy's lies as you follow His lead.

Instead of "have to's," Jesus offers Himself to you. Whenever you hear yourself admonishing you must or you have to, stop and consider all options. In doing so, you remind yourself you always have a choice and there are no "have to's." Prioritize spending time with Jesus, not just during set quiet times but at all times. Instead of doing it on your own or feeling alone, Jesus offers partnership and presence. Check in with Jesus throughout your day. You can ask for help and guidance and listen for His responses, or you can simply acknowledge His loving presence as He restores your peace and centers you on Him. Be Mary.

Instead of fear or selfishness, Jesus offers love as a guide for your choices. When faced with a choice, ask yourself, "What is the loving thing to do?" The answer to that question can help direct your steps to align with Christ's, because He always chose the loving thing. If you aren't sure what the loving thing is, ask Jesus to show you, and check in Scripture for other examples of loving choices and for descriptions of what love is and what love does.

CONCLUSION

The authority Christ has shared with you as His partner is precious and needs to be guarded and protected. Don't allow boundaries to be blurred, creating confusion and hindering your agency. Remember, any interruption in agency causes a wound in your soul. Owning your own choices, not allowing others to take over your choice-making, taking responsibility for the consequences of your own choices but not the choices of others, and not trying to own or make the choices of others protect your authority.

Your God-ordained right to choose is the fulcrum of your freedom in Christ. Because you have been given authority, you are:

Free to focus on Jesus first, above all else, knowing all else is of lesser importance;

Free to accept both the good consequences and the painful consequences of your choices, knowing He accepts you and loves you no matter what you choose;

Free to follow your true heart's desires and live from your true identity, because you have the right to choose to do so;

Free to walk in peace, knowing Christ is your partner who guards your heart and mind in His authority;

Free from the condemnation and judgments of others, knowing you have the right to choose for yourself, and you are responsible for your choices;

Free from fear, having confidence your partner is walking by your side in all you choose;

Free to love fully and to love well, as love is your guiding principle in all your choices.

Peace comes exercising your authority, your God-given right to choose, from a position of partnership with Jesus with love as your guide. Hope comes from knowing you always have another choice. The precious treasure of your authority is the pivotal piece of the map on your quest for the Kingdom life.

STARTING POINT: QUESTIONS TO EXPLORE AUTHORITY

Answer the following questions to further explore your God-ordained authority. Consider your answers prayerfully and thoughtfully. Don't offer a superficial response and move on to the next question but look deeply within and be as honest with yourself as you can be. Avoid giving "pat" answers you might have heard in church, particularly if you've not examined what those responses mean in depth. These questions are designed to help you understand your authority, and to begin to explore how to make Kingdom choices.

1. What are some ways you have exercised your authority?
2. What are some examples of times your authority was impeded or usurped?
3. How has the enemy tempted you to doubt your authority?
4. What are some examples of times you were angry or frustrated with God because you believed He should "control" your circumstances?

5. In what ways have boundaries in your life been blurred?
6. What feelings are stirred in you when you feel responsible for someone else's feelings or choices?
7. What feelings are stirred in you when you take responsibility for your feelings and choices?
8. What are some examples of times you have chosen like Mary? Martha?
9. How often have you made your choices based on believing you "had to"?
10. What are some examples of choices you have made based on love? What are some examples of choices you have made from a self-focus?

DESTINATION: PRAYERS TO UNCOVER AUTHORITY

Find a quiet place with few distractions to sit with Jesus. Still your mind and quiet your heart by repeating a verse of Scripture meaningful to you; for example, you could repeat, "He was given authority, glory, and sovereign power; all nations and peoples of every language worshiped him" (Daniel 7:14). I have written a prayer for you as an example, but use your own words, from your heart, to ask Jesus to uncover and renew your authority: *Lord, you say you have given me authority to overcome all the power of the enemy. Sometimes, though, I feel like other things overpower me and I seem to lose my ability to choose. Instead, I react to the people and circumstances around me. I would like to live fully in the authority You have given me. Would you please help me see and understand my authority?*

After you pray, spend time in silent meditation, eyes closed and listening for His answers. He may show you an image in your mind, or you may hear words or phrases in your mind describing or explaining your authority. He might bring to mind a particular verse or story from Scripture that reveals some aspect of your authority. You can recognize responses from the Lord by the peace they stir up in your heart. If an image or word comes to you that brings anxiety or shame, reject it, recenter yourself on Jesus, and ask again. If you think you hear a response that contradicts Scripture, pray against enemy interference, recenter on Jesus, and ask again. Otherwise, don't analyze what comes up or question if it's the Lord. Instead, go with it and follow wherever He takes you. If you are getting "off base," He will let you know. Keep with it, asking Jesus to explain anything you don't understand and to show you more, until you feel He is finished.

If you don't hear anything, don't be concerned or frustrated. Remember, we have an enemy who actively opposes our treasure seeking and tries to thwart our connection with Jesus. Take a break and come back to your prayer later. This time, if you don't receive a response, ask Jesus what is in the way. It may be a lie you believe, such as you are powerless, or you should or have to do something, or it may be distractions of life he is using to get in your way. False beliefs about God can also hinder making a connection; for example, seeing God as controlling, or distant and uncaring. Whatever Jesus reveals is in the way, ask Him to bring truth to your heart to move the hindrance out of your way. Then return to your prayer request.

Another prayer could be to ask Jesus for help with identifying who owns a specific problem. For example, you could pray: *Lord, I am confused in this situation. I'm being blamed/shamed for something that happened, but I don't know if I am responsible or not. Would you please show me who owns the problem?* Depending on the situation, He might show you where you are responsible, He might show you the part you are responsible for, or He may show you that you hold no responsibility, and that this is a situation where someone else has made the choice, so you do not own the problem at all. Be open to what He shows you. Be willing to accept any responsibility, ask forgiveness, and make amends as needed for any choices of yours which have caused hurt or pain. Be careful not to accept responsibility for things you did not choose but be willing to freely forgive the person who made the choice that hurt you.

Another approach you could take in prayer is to ask for help in choosing like Mary. Here is an example of a prayer asking for Mary's heart: *Lord, I know you said Mary chose what was better, and the only thing I need is You. But, Lord, the busyness, obligations, and responsibilities of life keep pressing in on me. Would you please show me how to choose like Mary and remain at Your feet?* Allow the Lord to reestablish peace in your heart. He may break down those things you feel obligated to do and help you prioritize, or He may urge you to let them go altogether. Be open to what He says and how He reveals what is important to you. It's alright to say to Him, *But Lord, it feels like I have to,* if He asks you to let things go but listen to His response after you express your feelings honestly. Follow up with a request to relieve you of the "have to" lie belief, by asking Him what the truth is about "have to's."

Finally, you can pray and ask Jesus to reveal where self-focus has taken over your choice-making. Self-focus can take the form of self-protection, self-debasement, self-centeredness, selfishness, self-defense, self-aggrandizement. The prayer could sound like this one: *Lord, I find myself making many of my choices based on what benefits me. I want to choose based on love, but sometimes I get caught up in protecting or defending myself, and I forget to ask what the loving choice would be. Would you please help me choose the loving thing when I make my choices?* When you choose based on self-motives, remember poor fruit grows from those roots of self. Allow Jesus to help you examine your motives. When you ask yourself, "what is the loving thing to do?" but are unsure what the loving thing is, turn to Jesus for clarity. Whatever He tells you is certainly the loving thing to choose.

Living from your God-given authority takes practice and intentionality. Pay attention to times you feel powerless or trapped. Notice particularly when you feel you are choosing based on fear. When those feelings arise, turn to Jesus in prayer, ask for His help to reestablish your authority, listen for whatever truth He wants to speak to your heart, and move forward based on His truth. Always partner with God in making your choices, which will help you stop choosing based on fear. Remember, your authority is precious. Guard it closely, with the Lord's help.

SETTING THE COURSE: LIVING YOUR AUTHORITY

The first section presents concepts you may want to internalize, and the second section lists some actions you may take to apply the information you have studied. Approach the following concepts and actions prayerfully. Avoid any thinking that you must rigidly adhere to them, because these are only suggestions and may not work for you. Everyone is different. Remember, you have authority over your choices of what you will believe, think, feel, and do. Use these suggestions to begin to build your own repertoire of tools and weapons you can use on your quest to live the Kingdom life.

INTERNALIZE THE CONCEPTS

Consider the importance of your authority. Meditate on the kind of love it would require for God to share His authority with you and choose to partner with you in creating the flow of life in this world.

Consider the value of keeping good, clear boundaries. Recognize how boundaries improve relationships by clarifying ownership of problems. Contemplate the importance of boundaries in keeping bulldozers out of your garden and keeping you from weeding other people's gardens.

Consider how taking responsibility for your choices is directly connected to your freedom. Evaluate the importance of taking responsibility for your choices and not taking responsibility for the choices, actions, or feelings of others. Reflect on how taking responsibility for others binds you to them and gives them power over you.

Consider the freedom provided by God, allowing you to always choose again. Contemplate how making a different choice while forgiving yourself, as God forgives you, for any poor choice allows for your growth and change.

Imagine choosing like Mary. Consider the feelings such a choice could stir in you. Examine what would need to change in your life to choose like Mary.

Imagine removing fear as a factor in your decision-making. Contemplate what would change in your life if you consistently chose based on love instead of self-serving purposes.

PROCESS THEIR APPLICATION

Remind yourself each day that you have authority to choose for yourself, and that authority is given to you by God, so no one, including the enemy, has the right to take it away (Luke 10:19).

As you make each choice during your day, use the language of choice. For example, instead of simply getting out of bed, say, "I choose to get up now." Instead of brushing your teeth without a thought, say, "I choose to brush my teeth now."

For each choice you make, consider all options and their consequences (Galatians 6:4). For example, when choosing what to eat, don't pick the first thing you see. Consider first what you desire to eat. Go over multiple options, then consider the consequences of each of those options. Think of short-term and long-term consequences. Then say, "I choose to eat _____."

When faced with what feels like a "have to" to you, stop before you act. Recall the truth that you have infinite choices. List as many choices as you can think of, any those you would not want to choose. For example, you have run out of diapers and "have to" go to the store to get more. (Of course, this happens at midnight, as all parents are aware.) Instead of jumping in the car in disgruntled frustration, stop and say, "I could go to buy diapers. I could use a bath cloth and wrap around him. I could let him sleep naked and clean it up in the morning. I could pack him up and head to the airport to fly to Minnesota. I could leave the wet diaper on him. I could go get myself a cheeseburger." Yes, some of those choices are ridiculous, but that's the point. Come up with as many as you can, then ask yourself, "But, what do I *want* to choose?" You will find it feels very different to go to the store for diapers because you want to instead of because you have to.

When you feel like interjecting your opinion into a conversation, ask yourself, "Am I invited?" If not, keep your opinion to yourself. When others want your opinion, they will ask for it (Proverbs 18:2).

When you find yourself wanting to control or influence someone else's choices, ask yourself, "Is this a weed in my garden?" If the problem or choice belongs to someone else, it isn't your weed and it isn't your garden. I often say, "Not my weed, not my garden," just to emphasize to myself I don't have a say over someone else's choices.

When a problem arises between you and someone else, ask yourself, "Who owns this problem?" If you identify something you have chosen that created or impacted the issue, take responsibility, ask forgiveness, and make amends as appropriate for any hurt or pain caused (Matthew 5:23-24). However, if you did not make the choice, allow the problem to belong to the other individual. One good way to tell if you own the problem is to ask, "If I was the one choosing right now, would I make this choice?" If the answer is no, you do not own the problem, because you would be choosing differently.

When you make a choice and you don't like the choice or the consequences of the choice, say to yourself, "I can always make another choice, because God has given me that right." Remind yourself of Jesus' forgiveness of you, paid for on the cross, and forgive yourself, then choose again, making a different choice this time.

When you feel tempted to choose based on fear, listen to what fear tells you to do, then do the opposite (I John 4:18). I call this the 180 degrees rule. If fear tells you to go north, turn and walk south. At least you will know you are walking closer to where God is going than you would if you listened to fear.

Establish a routine of spending time connecting with Jesus several times each day (I Thessalonians 5:17). It doesn't have to be first thing in the morning or the last thing before you go to bed, nor does it have to be time spent away or in a prayer closet or on your knees. You can choose to eat outside at lunch, enjoying His presence as you experience His creation. You can choose to talk to Him as you drive to work or as you prepare a meal. You can listen to Him as you clean your house. Listening to music, particularly music with meaningful words of a Christian theme, can help connect you to Jesus. You can ask for His help as you sort through a thorny problem at work or as you discipline your children. You can sit silently with Him without talking about anything, just relishing His loving presence. You can ask Him for input about every choice you make. All of these, and more, are options. Keep in mind, He just wants to be with you.

THREE

The Treasure of Indwelling

YOUR COMPASS

I pray that out of his glorious riches he may strengthen you with power through his Spirit in your inner being, so that Christ may dwell in your hearts through faith. And I pray that you, being rooted and established in love, may have power, together with all the Lord's holy people, to grasp how wide and long and high and deep is the love of Christ, and to know this love that surpasses knowledge—that you may be filled to the measure of all the fullness of God (Ephesians 3:16-19).

I will ask the Father, and he will give you another advocate to help you and be with you forever – the Spirit of truth. The world cannot accept him, because it neither sees him nor knows him. But you know him, for he lives with you and will be in you. On that day you will realize that I am in my Father, and you are in me, and I am in you. But the Advocate, the Holy Spirit, whom the Father will send in

*my name, will teach you all things and will remind you of
everything I have said to you (John 14:16-17, 20, 26).*

*Do you not know that your bodies are temples of the Holy Spirit,
who is in you, whom you have received from God? You are not your
own; you were bought at a price (I Corinthians 6:19-20).*

*When you believed, you were marked in him with a seal, the
promised Holy Spirit, who is a deposit guaranteeing our
inheritance until the redemption of those who are God's
possession—to the praise of his glory (Ephesians 1:13-14).*

*There are different kinds of gifts, but the same Spirit distributes
them. There are different kinds of service, but the same Lord. There
are different kinds of working, but in all of them and in everyone it
is the same God at work. Now to each one the manifestation of the
Spirit is given for the common good (I Corinthians 12:4-7).*

*But the fruit of the Spirit is love, joy, peace, forbearance, kindness,
goodness, faithfulness, gentleness and self-control (Galatians 5:22-
23).*

*Those who live in accordance with the Spirit have their minds set on
what the Spirit desires. You, however, are not in the realm of the
flesh but are in the realm of the Spirit, if indeed the Spirit of God
lives in you. And if anyone does not have the Spirit of Christ, they
do not belong to Christ. But if Christ is in you, then even though
your body is subject to death because of sin, the Spirit gives
life because of righteousness. And if the Spirit of him who raised*

Jesus from the dead is living in you, he who raised Christ from the dead will also give life to your mortal bodies because of his Spirit who lives in you. For those who are led by the Spirit of God are the children of God. The Spirit you received does not make you slaves, so that you live in fear again; rather, the Spirit you received brought about your adoption to sonship. And by him we cry, "Abba, Father." The Spirit himself testifies with our spirit that we are God's children (Romans 8:5, 9-11, 14-16).

MAP KEY: NEVER ALONE

INDWELLING DEFINED

*Y*ou are in Him and He is in you.

Well, that certainly sounds like that might be a good thing, but what does it really mean? Jesus sums up the crucial nature of the treasure of His indwelling with one simple phrase: "the kingdom of God is in your midst" (also translated, "within you") (Luke17:21). I don't think many fully appreciate the significance of His statement. When He comes to dwell within you, He brings the Kingdom – His presence *is* the Kingdom. In other words, you carry the Kingdom of God within you. The Kingdom of God is not some future to hope for, not some other place for you to get to, not something you hope to receive. The Kingdom of God is right here, right now. Jesus has accomplished this. It is your present reality.

To indwell means to abide within, as a guiding force, or to inhabit. Where the Temple was God's dwelling place on earth, the place where the Jews came to meet God, through Christ you are now "a dwelling in which God lives by His Spirit" (Ephesians 2:22). No longer do you have to trek to Jerusalem to come close to God. His home is within you.

These words aren't new. You've heard many times, I'm sure, about inviting Jesus into your heart. And like I said, that sounds good. Yet, how many live with Jesus as their personal, individual guiding force? How many experience unity and partnership with Him from within?

Here's a little test for you. When you talk about or think about God, do you look up or point to the sky? Do you pray up and out to God? If you do, your unconscious belief is still that God is up there somewhere – up in heaven, perhaps, or above, some distance from you. Yet, Jesus says clearly those who accept Him know Him, and He lives in them (John 14:17).

Jesus is in the Father in the same way you are in Him and He is in you. As God, Jesus, and the Holy Spirit are one, so are you one with Jesus. This miraculous and mysterious unity was bought and paid for on the cross. You don't have to wait to see Jesus when you die; He's already here. You don't have to search for Jesus or try to find Him; He's within you all the time. His Spirit, residing in your heart, is there to be your guide and partner right now.

So, what does it mean to partner with God? Throughout Scripture, the story is told of God's choice to partner with His creation in bringing about His will. Starting with Adam, God chose to work with and through humankind. The most significant partnership was between God and Abraham. God made His

76

covenant with Abraham to give him descendants and make him the father of many nations, to give him and his descendants a land of their own, and that through his lineage, all humanity would be saved. This promise of salvation for all, of course, refers to Jesus.

Another great example (among many) of God's partnership with man is seen in the story of Moses. God chose Moses to stand before Pharaoh and demand he free the slaves, to lead the children of Israel out of slavery in Egypt across the Red Sea, and to receive God's law. Could God have freed Israel without Moses? Of course. He could've supernaturally raised Israel out of Egypt and transplanted them in the land of promise. He could've wiped Egypt off the map with a wave of His hand, if He so desired. Instead, God provided the authority and power, and Moses participated as His partner to fulfill God's purposes. Yes, God could've done it all without Moses, but instead He chose partnership.

Notice in Moses' story how it mattered what Moses and the people of Israel did and didn't choose to do. Remember, Moses was resistant at first. God responded by giving him Aaron (Exodus 6:30-7:2). When Moses listened to God and spoke to Pharaoh as God told him to do, God demonstrated His power before all of Egypt until Pharaoh relented and set Israel free (Exodus 7:14-12:30). Pharaoh then pursued his former slaves, and once again, Moses followed God's direction, and God parted the sea for them to walk through on dry land (Exodus 14:5-22). When Israel later chose to create and worship a golden calf like the gods of Egypt, God was ready to bring disaster upon the "stiff-necked people," but Moses pleaded, making the case for them based on God's covenant with Abraham, and God changed His mind (Exodus 32:9-14). Do you see the significance of the choices of the people in partnership with God?

Scripture reveals how, from Adam to the disciples and Paul, every step of the way, God has chosen to partner with humankind. Notice the significant impacts those partnerships had on the individuals involved and beyond. The same is true today. He partners with you just like He partnered with so many others in Scriptural stories. When you are willing, and you stand in agreement with Him, He moves in authority and power in your life, which facilitates the process of transformation. You cannot help but be changed by the indwelling presence of God. Paul calls it having "the mind of Christ" (I Corinthians 2:16), and "being transformed into his image with ever-increasing glory, which comes from the Lord, who is the Spirit" (II Corinthians 3:18).

Through His indwelling Spirit, you also can understand the truth of Christ, as Paul explains: "these are the things God has revealed to us by his Spirit. The Spirit searches all things, even the deep things of God. For who knows a person's thoughts except their own spirit within them? In the same way no one knows the thoughts of God except the Spirit of God. What we have received is not the spirit of the world, but the Spirit who is from God, so that we may understand what God has freely given us. The person without the Spirit does not accept the things that come from the Spirit of God but considers them foolishness and cannot understand them because they are discerned only through the Spirit" (I Corinthians 2:10-12, 14). According to Jesus, it is the "Spirit of truth" who "will guide you into all truth" (John 16:13). Only by partnering with His indwelling Spirit can we comprehend and live fully in the truth of Christ.

You are "united with Christ" (Philippians 2:1) by His indwelling Spirit. On the night He was arrested, Jesus prayed for all believers, "that all of them may be one, Father, just as you are in me and I am in you. May they also be in us so that the world may believe that you have sent me. I have given them the glory that you gave me, that they may be one as we are one— I in them and you in me—so that they may be brought to complete unity" (John 17:21-23). Jesus is clear His desire is to abide in you as God is in Him. Paul confirms Jesus accomplished the fulfillment of this desire, saying, "whoever is united with the Lord is one with Him in spirit" (I Corinthians 6:17). Because of His presence within you, you are brought into unity with Christ and are one with Him, just as He is one with the Father – one mind, one heart, one spirit. Take a moment and contemplate this astounding truth.

UNITY WITH THE SPIRIT

In Romans 8:5-17, Paul describes the results of living in unity with the Spirit. He tells us that "those who live in accordance with the Spirit have their minds set on what the Spirit desires" (verse 5). To truly have your mind set on what His Spirit desires, you need to be in continuous connection and communication with Him, at all times and about all things. You can no longer rely on your own perceptions, interpretations, opinions, viewpoints, past experiences, or present circumstances to inform your thoughts and feelings.

You are used to relying on your physical senses to interpret and understand the world, but physical senses cannot "see" in the spiritual realm. To be "taught by the Spirit, explaining spiritual realities with Spirit-taught words" (I Corinthians 2:13), you need to see through the Spirit's eyes, interpret only through His truth, and formulate your views and opinions based on what you hear Him saying and what you know He has said and done. Just as Jesus did only what He saw His Father doing (John 5:19), you seek to see what Jesus is doing within you and follow in one accord. When you live in unity with the Spirit, you no longer give weight to this physical "reality" that your senses perceive. Your reality becomes His reality, giving all weight to the spiritual truth your spirit perceives through the presence of His Spirit in you.

As a result, your circumstances no longer have power over your feelings, but instead it is His presence, His love for you, and His peace that influences your feelings. This is how Paul was able to "give thanks in all circumstances" (I Thessalonians 5:18) and how he "learned to be content whatever the circumstances" (Philippians 4:11). Your reality becomes Christ's reality. You see as He sees. You know only what He knows. Your heart can remain in peace always, despite difficult circumstances. Paul describes it this way: "The mind governed by the flesh is death, but the mind governed by the Spirit is life and peace" (Romans 8:6).

Even the physical reality of death loses its power. As Paul explains in Romans 8:10, "But if Christ is in you, then even though your body is subject to death because of sin, the Spirit gives life because of righteousness." So even death has no power in your life. In the same way, all aspects of the "flesh" lose power as you live in accordance with the Spirit. As you agree to partner with Him, your desires, which were once tied to gratifying your physical body and worldly beliefs and feelings, such as fear and shame, become the Spirit's desires, fulfilled by Him, seeking only the things of His Kingdom. As Galatians 5:16 states, "So I say, walk by the Spirit, and you will not gratify the desires of the flesh."

80

When you choose to partner with Jesus, allow Him to have authority in your life, and are willing for Him to do His work in you, He makes transformational changes in the deepest places in your heart, such that your root values and beliefs come to match His own, and your motivations and purposes in life arise from His truth. Paul explains this deep-level change in Romans 8:7-9 in this way: "The mind governed by the flesh is hostile to God; it does not submit to God's law, nor can it do so. Those who are in the realm of the flesh cannot please God. You, however, are not in the realm of the flesh but are in the realm of the Spirit, if indeed the Spirit of God lives in you." And Paul goes on, in Romans 12:2, to instruct us, "Do not conform to the pattern of this world but be transformed by the renewing of your mind. Then you will be able to test and approve what God's will is—his good, pleasing and perfect will." Your role in this transformation is to willingly invite Jesus to change you (He will do nothing against your will) and submit to how He wants to work. Your agreement with Him allows Him to exercise His power and authority within you.

The deeper things of the heart, the things underlying the surface actions or behaviors, like motivations, values, purpose, and foundational beliefs, are like the roots of the tree, while actions are the leaves and branches. When you focus on changing the surface things like behaviors, words, results, and outcomes, you become like a gardener who prunes branches and cuts back leaves, but the "tree" itself continues to grow back year after year, so nothing really changes. The indwelling of His Spirit allows you to go deeper, under the surface, where your "fruit" actually is determined.

The foundational desire of your flesh, born from Adam and Eve's desire in the garden to "be like God, knowing good and evil"

(Genesis 3:5), is the desire to be god of your own life. From this sin of the flesh, the sin nature is born. It is the root of all sin behaviors. The desire to be your own god must be broken in order to be put to death within you. It is in this place of brokenness, where your desire to be your own god dies, that you can find who you really are, and where you can finally and truly be free.

When you receive His Spirit to dwell within you, you are agreeing to exchange your desire to be your own god for reliance on Christ. Apart from God, however, it is impossible to destroy this root of self as god. When you approach God from a position of need, acknowledging your inability with humility and expressing your willingness for Him to partner with you in breaking the desire to be like God, His Spirit is empowered to cut down the root of the desires of the flesh, leaving room for what the Spirit plants within you to grow and produce good fruit. You become a "new creation" (II Corinthians 5:17), and nothing else counts but the new creation (Galatians 6:15). Whatever root remains planted in you produces fruit. The question is, will it be the old root of the desires of the flesh, or will it be the new seeds, planted by the Holy Spirit in the good soil of your heart?

FRUIT OF THE SPIRIT

The indwelling of the Spirit produces certain fruit in your life. These fruits of the Spirit are "love, joy, peace, forbearance, kindness, goodness, faithfulness, gentleness and self-control" (Galatians 5:22-23). Paul goes on to say, "Against such things there is no law. Those who belong to Christ Jesus have crucified the flesh with its passions and desires. Since we live by the Spirit, let us keep in step with the Spirit" (Galatians 5:23-25). Notice the direct

82

connection made between "crucifying the flesh with its passions and desires" (in other words, breaking the desire to be your own god) and the presence of the fruit of the Spirit.

Paul begins the list of the fruit of the Spirit with love, for good reason. Jesus identified love as the greatest commandment: "Love the Lord your God with all your heart and with all your soul and with all your mind and with all your strength...Love your neighbor as yourself. There is no commandment greater than these" (Mark 12:30-31). Paul calls love, "the greatest of these" (I Corinthians 13:13). I John 4:7-8 &12 states: "Dear friends, let us love one another, for love comes from God. Everyone who loves has been born of God and knows God. Whoever does not love does not know God, because God is love. No one has ever seen God; but if we love one another, God lives in us and his love is made complete in us." In other words, God's own nature is love, and when He dwells within you, you will reflect His nature. His love makes your love complete.

I Corinthians 13, often called the "love" chapter of the Bible, also reveals how crucial the fruit of love is to God. "If I speak in the tongues of men or of angels, but do not have love, I am only a resounding gong or a clanging cymbal. If I have the gift of prophecy and can fathom all mysteries and all knowledge, and if I have a faith that can move mountains, but do not have love, I am nothing. If I give all I possess to the poor and give over my body to hardship that I may boast, but do not have love, I gain nothing" (verses 1-3). Love is the key, the centerpiece of all, and what you do, if not undergirded and motivated by love, means nothing. Without love, you have nothing of meaning or importance. The Kingdom is made of the substance of love.

What is love? Love is often defined in terms of what you "do" or how you "feel," but it is more a state of being than an action or emotion. Love is a motive of the heart. C. S. Lewis describes it this way: "Love is not affectionate feeling, but a steady wish for the loved person's ultimate good as far as it can be obtained."[1] It is important not to confuse the evidence of love with love itself. Paul goes on in I Corinthians 13:4-8 to describe love based on the attitudes created by its presence, but again, he does not assume to define love here, just to describe its fruit. It is interesting to note that Paul, in his description of love, included some of the fruits of the Spirit as evidence of the presence of love, further revealing the primary importance of love among the spiritual fruit and the all-encompassing nature of love as the "being" of God rather than as a set of actions or feelings in response to another. Love is the very presence of God, and the outflow of love behaves as His presence behaves.

The cross is the love of God displayed. Jesus saw your sin, not generically but personally, looking one-on-one into your eyes and knowing every aspect and fiber of your being and each and every sin of commission and omission, as well as the exact cost of each of those individual sins, and He wept over the inevitable death that your sin produces in you. Rather than see that death realized, He wrenched that sin off of you and grappled with it Himself, eye to eye, face to face, hand to hand (literally). He absorbed your death, the one you rightly deserved, and anguished through it on your behalf. He didn't ever have to know death, but He still chose to experience death in its most horrific expression, for your sake. The alternative that you faced, which was permanent suffering, was untenable for Him who loved you so dearly.

84

The cross, the most powerful and perfect symbol of sacrifice known, is the example Christ set for you, His demonstration of His love. He knew what you truly needed for your ultimate good, and He met that need as only He could. But don't interpret sacrifice to mean you are to demean or degrade yourself, as if you don't matter. You are not to forget who you are for the sake of another or lose yourself in their lives. Jesus never forgot Who He was, and He never degraded His life, His worth, or His importance. Instead, He chose based on exactly Who He was. He chose based on love freely given.

If you have the mind of Christ, you seek to understand the genuine need and best interest of those you love, and as you are able, seek to meet their ultimate good to the best of your ability. That is a true picture of sacrifice. You are still completely who you are, with your own needs and dreams, and from the heart of your true nature, you willingly give of yourself, never seeing it as a loss because you gave by your own choice based on your own desire. Regarding laying down His life, Jesus said, "No one takes it from me, but I lay it down of my own accord" (John 10:18). As is seen in these words, love is sacrifice willingly and freely given, without expectation of return – given for the ultimate good of the heart of the other, from the true desire of your heart.

The cross reveals, then, something important about the nature of love. Love is directly opposed to self as god. Love denies the self, takes up the cross, and follows Christ (Luke 9:23). Again, can you see how the desire to be your own god must be broken for this fruit of His Spirit to be revealed in you? Love and self as god cannot coexist.

Paul describes the importance of humility in love when he writes: "Therefore if you have any encouragement from being united with Christ, if any comfort from his love, if any common sharing in the Spirit, if any tenderness and compassion, then make my joy complete by being like-minded, having the same love, being one in spirit and of one mind. Do nothing out of selfish ambition or vain conceit. Rather, in humility value others above yourselves, not looking to your own interests but each of you to the interests of the others. In your relationships with one another, have the same mindset as Christ Jesus" (Philippians 2:1-5). Through the Spirit's indwelling, as you are willing, you are enabled to have the mind of Christ, who always chooses from a motive of love, and His love is empowered to flow through you to others.

In the same way love is opposed to self as god, love and fear cannot exist together. Scripture teaches, "There is no fear in love. But perfect love drives out fear" (I John 4:18). When you live in the Kingdom through the indwelling of His Spirit, fear has no place in you, and you no longer make your choices based on fear. Romans 8:15 states, "The Spirit you received does not make you slaves, so that you live in fear again; rather, the Spirit you received brought about your adoption to sonship." Fear in all its forms – worry, anxiety, panic, self-protection, defensiveness, and control – are not part of God's Kingdom, because the Kingdom is rooted and grounded in love.

Of love, Paul says it "does not envy, it does not boast, it is not proud. It is not rude, it is not self-seeking, it is not easily angered, it keeps no record of wrongs. Love does not delight in evil but rejoices with the truth. It always protects, always trusts, always hopes, always perseveres" (I Corinthians 13:4-7). However, that doesn't mean love accepts everything and never confronts or disagrees with anything. In fact, the example Jesus set in His interactions with the Pharisees and teachers of the law was loving confrontation. To allow them to continue in their hypocrisy without bringing it to their attention would not have been loving them well.

Galatians 6:1 says it clearly: "Brothers, if someone is caught in a sin, you who are spiritual should restore him gently." II Timothy 2:25 teaches to "gently instruct" those who oppose the truth and goes on in 4:2 to charge you to "correct, rebuke and encourage—with great patience and careful instruction." Jesus demonstrated love in every area – with the prostitutes and tax collectors, with the Pharisees and teachers of the law, with Peter and with Paul. His confrontation and correction were just as much His love as was the cross.

Love is the source and foundation for all other fruits of the Spirit, which makes sense given the understanding that God is love. Joy abounds from allowing the love of God to fill you and flow freely into others and from sharing your love with God. Your joy in the Lord begins because of your salvation, as the psalmist wrote: "Come, let us sing for joy to the LORD; let us shout aloud to the Rock of our salvation," (Psalm 95:1) and continues in the fulfillment of God's healing of your heart as prophesied in Isaiah 61:1, 3: "The Spirit of the Sovereign LORD is on me, because the LORD has anointed me to proclaim good news to the poor. He has sent me to bind up the brokenhearted, to proclaim freedom for the captives…to bestow on them a crown of beauty instead of ashes, the oil of joy instead of mourning, and a garment of praise instead of a spirit of despair." What else but joy could flow from such wonderful provisions of God on your behalf? This joy multiplies when His love is shared freely with others.

The peace of God "transcends all understanding" (Philippians 4:7), no matter your circumstances, because His love is a stable and secure grounding in your life, a never-changing place where you can stand. His peace also becomes your shield, a guard over your heart and mind (Philippians 4:7). Whenever your peace is disrupted, you can know instantly that whatever caused the loss of peace is not of God or from God but is an imposition of the enemy. This awareness equips you to fight effectively against the enemy's schemes.

His love will "fill you with the knowledge of his will through all the wisdom and understanding that the Spirit gives" so that you will be "strengthened with all power according to his glorious might so that you may have great endurance and patience" (Colossians 1:9, 11). As Jesus shows great patience with you, never giving up on you and always forgiving you, His Spirit empowers you to greater and greater patience with the people in your life. You can begin to see others through His eyes, with greater compassion and understanding, as He shows them to you in the truth of who He created them to be.

The love of God fosters Christlikeness in you. Everyone wants to be like those they love. So, the kindness, gentleness, and goodness Jesus demonstrates toward you, in accepting you despite your failings (II Corinthians 8:12), loving you while you were still a sinner (Romans 5:8), and adopting you as His beloved child and giving you the riches of His full inheritance (Ephesians 1:13-14), becomes part of your heart and is expressed toward others out of your love for Him. Paul puts it this way: "Therefore, as God's chosen people, holy and dearly loved, clothe yourselves with compassion, kindness, humility, gentleness and patience" (Colossians 3:12). Remember, you are to have the same mindset as Christ (Philippians 2:5).

You might assume faithfulness is a choice rather than a fruit of the Spirit, and certainly, a decision to believe in Jesus is a choice; however, without the help of the Holy Spirit, you could not produce or maintain certainty in what you hope for or knowledge of unseen things (Hebrews 11:1). As the father of the boy possessed by an impure spirit said to Jesus, "I do believe; help me overcome my unbelief!" (Mark 9:24). You choose to believe and are empowered to do so through the presence of His Spirit. Do you see the partnership in operation?

The last fruit of the Spirit listed is self-control, translated in other versions as temperance, meaning balance, restraint, and moderation in action, thought, and feeling. Paul is referencing thoughtful, considered responses as opposed to extreme reactions and emotions. When you react to situations or other people's behaviors, you are giving power to the circumstance or action of the other and allowing that situation or action to determine your emotion and behavior. In doing so, you are giving away your authority. But when you are thoughtful and measured, giving a considered response, you are the one choosing your behavior and feelings, maintaining your authority.

Proverbs associates wisdom with restraint (Proverbs 17:27, 29:18) and great difficulty with a lack of self-control (Proverbs 25:28). Paul warns a lack of self-control opens you up to temptation from the enemy (I Corinthians 7:5). So, an attitude of restraint benefits you in many ways. According to Scripture, it is God's

89

grace that "teaches us to say 'No' to ungodliness and worldly passions, and to live self-controlled, upright and godly lives in this present age" (Titus 2:12). In other words, the love He shows through His grace and mercy inspires you to follow His example. Jesus demonstrates restraint in His limitless mercy.

Above all, you must always remember you cannot produce the fruit of the Spirit alone. All your best efforts to "do good" will fall far short, and since these efforts are not coming from an overflow of His love and the presence of His Spirit, they will not produce the desired results in you or in the world. Instead, it is "His divine power" which "has given us everything we need for a godly life through our knowledge of him who called us by his own glory and goodness" (II Peter 1:3). As you partner with Jesus, His Spirit indwelling in you produces the many fruits of love.

II Peter 1:4 continues to explain how God's "precious promises" make it possible for you to "participate in the divine nature," meaning to be transformed into the likeness of Christ. The author goes on to say "For if you possess these qualities (faithfulness, goodness, self-control, perseverance, and most importantly, love) in increasing measure, they will keep you from being ineffective and unproductive in your knowledge of our Lord Jesus Christ" (II Peter 1:5, 8).

THE GIFTS OF THE SPIRIT

In addition to the fruit of the Spirit, the indwelling of His Spirit brings certain gifts. These gifts are listed in several places in Scripture and are all given for the edification of the body of Christ. Every child of God is given a gift or gifts, but not everyone has the same gifts or all the gifts. Think of it this way: just as a soldier is trained and equipped for his or her role in the battle, you are gifted by God in the way you need to stand in the battle He has prepared you to fight. God promises to "equip you with everything good for doing his will" (Hebrews 13:21) and "so that the body of Christ may be built up" (Ephesians 4:12). In the same way you would not train a Navy Seal in the skills needed to fly a stealth bomber or teach a logistical administrator in charge of planning troop movements how to be a bomb disposal operator, you are gifted to match your purpose and role in the spiritual war. These gifts are His training, preparation, and equipping.

What are the gifts of the Spirit? The gifts take different forms, and each serves a specific function. As Paul explains in Romans 12: 4-8, "For just as each of us has one body with many members, and these members do not all have the same function, so in Christ we, though many, form one body, and each member belongs to all the others. We have different gifts, according to the grace given to each of us. If your gift is prophesying, then prophesy in accordance with your faith; if it is serving, then serve; if it is teaching, then teach; if it is to encourage, then give encouragement; if it is giving, then give generously; if it is to lead, do it diligently; if it is to show mercy, do it cheerfully." In addition to describing the gifts, these verses demonstrate how to attitude and motive – in other words, the heart – of the individual sharing the gift matters in the gift's execution and impact.

Similarly, in I Corinthians 12:4-11, the gifts of the Spirit are described as being given for the good of all. "There are different kinds of gifts, but the same Spirit distributes them. There are different kinds of service, but the same Lord. There are different kinds of working, but in all of them and in everyone it is the same

God at work. Now to each one the manifestation of the Spirit is given for the common good. To one there is given through the Spirit a message of wisdom, to another a message of knowledge by means of the same Spirit, to another faith by the same Spirit, to another gifts of healing by that one Spirit, to another miraculous powers, to another prophecy, to another distinguishing between spirits, to another speaking in different kinds of tongues, and to still another the interpretation of tongues. All these are the work of one and the same Spirit, and he distributes them to each one, just as he determines."

Prophesy and teaching are the two spiritual gifts mentioned in all three places where spiritual gifts are identified (Romans 12, I Corinthians 12, Ephesians 4). Paul included them in what he called "the greater gifts" (I Corinthians 12:31). It makes sense how prophesy and teaching are highlighted for bringing edification to the body of Christ. Yet, Paul makes it very clear "God has placed the parts in the body, every one of them, just as He wanted them to be" (I Corinthians 12:18), and each part is "indispensable" and "honorable" (I Corinthians 12:22-23).

When teaching about recognizing false prophets, Jesus said, "By their fruit you will recognize them. Do people pick grapes from thornbushes or figs from thistles? Likewise, every good tree bears good fruit, but a bad tree bears bad fruit" (Matthew 7:16-17). While spiritual gifts can be imitated or counterfeited, the same is not true of spiritual fruit. The motives of the heart produce the fruit that grows in your life, so there is no faking that. When His Spirit lives in your heart, He fosters in you the motive of love. Love is the revealing fruit by which all can recognize the children of God. "By this everyone will know that you are my disciples, if you love one another" (John 13:35).

Paul ends his discussion on the spiritual gifts with this conclusion: "And yet I will show you the most excellent way" (I Corinthians 12:31). What is the most excellent way? According to Paul, it is the way of love. All the gifts mean nothing without love. So, you have come full circle, back to the very nature of God within you. The indwelling of the Holy Spirit fills your heart to overflowing with love. As Jesus said, all the Law and the prophets are contained in this one word: love.

CONCLUSION

You can't change your flesh. You can't heal the wounds in your heart. You can't win in a battle against the enemy on your own. Yet, these truths don't bring despair, because you have a partner, His indwelling Spirit, and you are never alone. His heart and your heart are made one – an astonishing and humbling truth – by His choice to be ever-present and connected with you, unified in mind, heart, and spirit. Through His presence, joined with your willingness to partner with Him, your mind is transformed, the wounds of your heart are healed, your spirit is enlivened, and your motives grow to match His heart of love. His love then begins to produce certain fruit in you and provides you with equipping for the battle against evil, for the benefit of the body of Christ. Remember, you cannot produce the fruit of His Spirit on your own, nor can His gifts be activated from the motive of love without His love within you making it possible.

He guides you and guards your steps through your connected relationship and oneness with Him. Because of His indwelling Spirit, you are:

Free to experience the joy of the Lord and the strength arising from it;

Free to live in the peace beyond understanding, despite difficult circumstances and less-than-desired outcomes;

Free to extend His patient grace to others, because you see them through His eyes instead of through your own;

Free from worry about being "good enough" because you know you are accepted and loved by Him;

Free to believe with certainty, because you experience His presence first-hand;

Free from the extremes of fleshly reaction that produce regret or leave you vulnerable to unnecessary pain;

Free to partner with Jesus in walking out your life, each day and every moment.

Peace comes from knowing it is not all up to you, but you have a partner to walk through life with you and help you along the path. Joy comes from receiving His love, His comfort, and His truth in your spirit. The treasure of the unity of your spirit with His Spirit is priceless, worth selling all you own to possess.

STARTING POINT: QUESTIONS TO EXPLORE HIS INDWELLING

Answer the following questions to further explore your experiences of the indwelling of His Spirit. Consider your answers prayerfully and thoughtfully. Don't offer a superficial response and move on to the next question but look deeply within and be as honest with yourself as you can be. Avoid giving "pat" answers you might have heard in church, particularly if you've not examined what those responses mean in depth. These questions are designed to help you understand and experience His indwelling on a deeper level.

1. In what ways have you experienced the presence of His Spirit within you?
2. Where in your daily life do you invite Jesus to be your partner?
3. What are some places you are willing to invite His partnership that you have felt on your own to this point?
4. How would you describe your unity with Christ?
5. What changes has Jesus made in you through His presence?
6. What do you believe still needs to be changed by His presence?
7. In what ways is "self as god" still in evidence in your life?
8. What fruit of the Spirit do you see expressed in your day to day living?
9. What gifts of the Spirit have you been given? What do those gifts indicate about your role in the spiritual battle?
10. What motives can you recognize behind your actions and attitudes in your relationships with others?

DESTINATION: PRAYERS TO UNCOVER HIS INDWELLING

Find a quiet place with few distractions to sit with Jesus. Still your mind and quiet your heart by repeating a verse of Scripture meaningful to you; for example, you could repeat, "Remain in me, as I also remain in you" (John 15:4). I have written a prayer for you as an example, but use your own words, from your heart, to ask Jesus to deepen your awareness of His indwelling Spirit: *Lord, you say you are in me and I am in you. Sometimes, though, I feel a distance between us, like you are far away instead of real and present. I would like to fully experience the indwelling of your Spirit. Would you please deepen my awareness of your presence and help me see and experience you more completely?*

After you pray, spend time in silent meditation, eyes closed and listening for His answers. He may show you an image in your mind, or you may hear words or phrases in your mind, or you may sense emotions or experiences He brings to you to reveal His presence. He might bring to mind a particular verse or story from Scripture that reveals some aspect of His Spirit. You can recognize responses from the Lord by the peace they stir up in your heart. If an image or word comes to you that brings anxiety or shame, reject it, recenter yourself on Jesus, and ask again. If you think you hear a response that contradicts Scripture, pray against enemy interference, recenter on Jesus, and ask again. Otherwise, don't analyze what comes up or question if it's the Lord. Instead, go with it and follow wherever He takes you. If you are getting "off base," He will let you know. Keep with it, asking Jesus to explain anything you don't understand and to show you more, until you feel He is finished.

If you don't hear anything, don't be concerned or frustrated. Remember, we have an enemy who actively opposes our treasure seeking and tries to thwart our connection with Jesus. Take a break and come back to your prayer later. This time, if you don't receive a response, ask Jesus what is in the way. It may be a lie you believe, such as you are not worth loving or not good enough for Him to desire to live in you, or it may be distractions of life the enemy is using to get in your way. False beliefs about God can also hinder making a connection; for example, seeing God as controlling, or distant and uncaring. Whatever Jesus reveals is in the way, ask Him to bring truth to your heart to move the hindrance out of your way. Then return to your prayer request.

Another prayer you could pursue is asking Jesus to show you how to partner more effectively with Him. For example, you could pray: *Lord, I'm used to doing things on my own. I've always taken care of things myself, but I'm tired and overwhelmed, and I don't want to keep doing things that way. I am willing to partner with you. Would you teach me how to walk as your partner and include you in everything in my life?* Listen for His suggestions on how to practice partnership in your relationship with Him. He might give you an image symbolizing what it is like to walk through life in partnership with Him. He might offer you ways to remind yourself to do "check-ins" with Him on an ongoing basis, such as leaving notes on your mirror and computer screen saying, "Check with Jesus." Work with Him on adopting the methods you find most effective in helping you remain connected with Him in prayer on an ongoing basis. Remember, Scripture instructs us to "pray continually" (I Thessalonians 5:17).

Another area of focus for prayer would be to go with Him to those areas in your heart still in the process of transformation into the likeness of Christ and allow Him to continue to bring change. Your prayer could be, *"Lord, show me places in my heart you still want to bring transformation. I am willing to meet you in those places and allow you to make the changes you want to make in me. Help me see what you are doing and strengthen me to participate with you in making those changes."* The most likely elements Jesus will reveal from this prayer are lies you still believe, about yourself or about Him. He may also reveal attitudes and motives that don't match the fruit of the Spirit. Go with Him wherever He takes you, whether in memory or symbolic imagery or conversation, agree with Him on the changes He wants to bring, and walk with Him through the experiences He brings to your heart and mind to make those changes. Transformation is a process, so be willing to continue to walk through these experiences with Him until you feel the change is accomplished and you are at peace in that area.

Finally, you can seek from Jesus knowledge on the fruits of the Spirit and the gifts of the Spirit you have. Pray something like this: *"Lord, you promise your Spirit produces good fruit. Would you show me how the fruit of your Spirit is demonstrated in my life? You also promise to equip me with gifts for the war. Would you reveal my gifts to me and help me see how I am to use them in the battle?"* Go through each fruit on the list and ask Him to show you evidence of it in your daily life. Seek from Him additional places His spiritual fruit could be expressed. Then, ask Him which spiritual gifts you have, from the different lists in Scripture. He may tie together your gift(s) with His revelation of your identity from the earlier chapter, because our gifts are often connected to who He created us to be.

Don't try to "produce" fruit or spiritual giftings on your own. Always check with Him on the motives of your heart and ask Him to promote love as your primary motive for your thoughts, feelings, and actions. Always keep in mind, you are not alone. You

98

have a partner who lives within you, who loves you dearly and wants only to be with you and help you walk through this life. Pay attention to His presence, for what we focus our attention on is what we notice and experience. Remind yourself He is always there, and if you are not experiencing Him, quiet yourself, focus your heart and mind within, and open yourself up to Him. His indwelling Spirit will never leave you on your own.

SETTING THE COURSE: LIVING IN HIS INDWELLING

The first section presents concepts you may want to internalize, and the second section lists some actions you may take to apply the information you have studied. Approach the following concepts and actions prayerfully. Avoid any thinking that you must rigidly adhere to them, because these are only suggestions and may not work for you. Everyone is different. Remember, it isn't up to you to "make" transformation or spiritual fruit happen. Use these suggestions to deepen your reliance on Him in your quest to live the Kingdom life.

INTERNALIZE THE CONCEPTS

Consider the importance of your oneness with Jesus. Meditate on the boundless love God has for you to choose to unite with you as one mind, one heart, and one spirit.

Consider the implications of having the "mind of Christ." Contemplate any areas where your mind remains worldly and consider granting God the opportunity to transform and renew your mind to come into agreement with His. Reflect on truths He brings to your heart and mind as you invite Him to bring change.

Consider the role of your willingness in growing in oneness with Christ. Examine your willingness to go to the deeper places of your heart and to allow Him to break the root of self as god in you. Contemplate what you desire to hold onto from the desire to be your own god (for example, self-protection, self-determination, etc.) and evaluate your willingness to surrender those things in humility to God.

Consider how your motives impact the presence of the fruit of the Spirit in your life. Examine your motives and evaluate when and how often the motive of love directs your path.

Examine your life for evidence of the fruit of the Spirit. Consider what beliefs you continue to hold in your heart that hinder the flow of the fruit of the Spirit and examine your willingness to partner with Jesus to change those beliefs to His truth. Imagine how your relationships might change if the fruit of the Spirit flowed freely in your life.

Meditate on how your spiritual gifts can be used to edify the body of Christ. Consider how you can partner with Jesus to use your spiritual gifts in warfare against the enemy.

PROCESS THEIR APPLICATION

Begin each day reaffirming your choice to live in partnership with Jesus. Invite Jesus to help direct your steps and check with Him at each choice you make to see what His thoughts and feelings are about your choice. Prayerfully make your decisions together.

When you notice a response, in either emotion or thought or behavior, contrary to the "mind of Christ," ask Jesus to show you the source of the response in you. Then, once the "root" source is identified, seek truth through prayer. Ask Jesus to reveal what you need to know to remove the root and ask Him to plant the truth in its place. When the truth is revealed, apply His truth to the situation that stirred the initial response.

Spend time getting to know Jesus. Talk with Him about anything and everything, from the mundane to the serious, from the inconsequential to the substantial. Also, seek shared experiences with Jesus. Some examples might be to take a walk with Him or lie on a hillside and watch the clouds with Him. Choose something you enjoy. As you share the experience with Him, listen and watch for His responses to you and to the experience you are sharing. Open your heart to feel His feelings in the moment and share your feelings with Him.

If you feel some resistance to change you are aware Jesus is trying to bring about (for example, if you have some fleshly behavior you don't want to give up, but you feel He is working to remove the desire for it, and you find yourself resisting His help), prayerfully ask Jesus to reveal where your unwillingness is rooted. While on the surface it may appear you just don't want to change, it is likely there is a deeper, hidden reason for your resistance. You might think you are "getting something good" from the behavior. You might be trying to "be in control" which grows out of the root of self as god. Whatever He reveals, ask Him to help you in your unwillingness by bringing whatever truth you need. If you are not willing to ask for His help, ask for His forgiveness and seek His response in your heart.

Actively seek opportunities for the fruit of the Spirit to be expressed from within you. Again, this doesn't look like "trying" to be loving or "trying" to be joyful. When opportunities arise where you might express love or joy, or any of the other fruit, ask Jesus to produce the fruit and help it to flow from you. Ask Him to remove obstacles to its expression.

Once you know your spiritual gifts, ask Jesus to reveal where and how He would suggest employing those gifts. If you have the gift of prophesy, be bold and speak truth when Jesus prompts your spirit that truth is needed. If you have the gift of teaching, prayerfully seek a place you can teach others (it doesn't have to be in a classroom or with a group) Be open and let Him be creative about where your gift can be best utilized.

FOUR

The Treasure of Protection

YOUR COMPASS

*He is a shield to those whose walk is blameless, for he guards the
course of the just and protects the way of his faithful ones. Then you
will understand what is right and just and fair—every good
path. For wisdom will enter your heart, and knowledge will be
pleasant to your soul. Discretion will protect you, and
understanding will guard you (Proverbs 2:7-11).*

*We are hard pressed on every side, but not crushed; perplexed, but
not in despair; persecuted, but not abandoned; struck down, but not
destroyed. We always carry around in our body the death of
Jesus, so that the life of Jesus may also be revealed in our
body. Therefore, we do not lose heart. Though outwardly we are
wasting away, yet inwardly we are being renewed day by day. For
our light and momentary troubles are achieving for us an eternal
glory that far outweighs them all (II Corinthians 4:8-10, 16-17).*

103

Whoever dwells in the shelter of the Most High will rest in the shadow of the Almighty. I will say of the LORD, "He is my refuge and my fortress, my God, in whom I trust." Surely, he will save you from the fowler's snare and from the deadly pestilence. He will cover you with his feathers, and under his wings you will find refuge; his faithfulness will be your shield and rampart. "Because he loves me," says the LORD, "I will rescue him; I will protect him, for he acknowledges my name. He will call on me, and I will answer him; I will be with him in trouble, I will deliver him and honor him" (Psalm 91:1-4, 14-15).

My prayer is not that you take them out of the world but that you protect them from the evil one (John 17:15).

But you, LORD, are a shield around me, my glory, the One who lifts my head high. I call out to the LORD, and he answers me from his holy mountain (Psalm 3:3-4).

God will speak to this people, to whom he said, "This is the resting place, let the weary rest"; and, "This is the place of repose"— but they would not listen. You boast, "We have entered into a covenant with death, with the realm of the dead we have made an agreement. When an overwhelming scourge sweeps by, it cannot touch us, for we have made a lie our refuge and falsehood our hiding place." So this is what the Sovereign LORD says: "See, I lay a stone in Zion, a tested stone, a precious cornerstone for a sure foundation; the one who relies on it will never be stricken with panic. I will make justice the measuring line and righteousness the plumb line; hail will sweep away your refuge, the lie, and water will overflow your hiding place. Your covenant with death will be annulled; your agreement with the realm of the dead will not stand." (Isaiah 28:11-12, 15-18).

Therefore, put on the full armor of God, so that when the day of evil comes, you may be able to stand your ground, and after you have done everything, to stand. Stand firm then, with the belt of truth buckled around your waist, with the breastplate of righteousness in place, and with your feet fitted with the readiness that comes from the gospel of peace. In addition to all this, take up the shield of faith, with which you can extinguish all the flaming arrows of the evil one. Take the helmet of salvation and the sword of the Spirit, which is the word of God (Ephesians 6:13-17).

MAP KEY: SWORD AND SHIELD

PROTECTION DEFINED

*J*esus is your sure foundation.

He is your place of refuge, your shelter, your sword and your shield. Does that mean nothing bad will ever happen to you, that you will not have difficulty in your life or pain and suffering to face? Ask Paul and the apostles. All except John met with painful, torturous deaths because they followed Jesus.

Jesus did not promise to prevent difficulties. In fact, He said, "In this world, you will have trouble" (John 16:33). He warned the disciples they would be hated and persecuted because they followed Him (Matthew 10:22 and 24:9). So, clearly, protection is not defined by God as preventing bad things from happening.

Rather than prevent difficulty, Jesus is present in the difficulty with you. God didn't prevent Joseph from being sold into slavery or being falsely accused of rape; instead, He remained with Joseph while he was in Egypt and helped him gain favor, then turned his presence there for good. God walks through the deep waters with you and goes before you as fire and cloud, like He did with Moses and the children of Israel. Pharaoh and the soldiers of Egypt still came, but their apparent might had no power before God.

Jesus walks through the furnace with you, like He did with Shadrach, Meshach, and Abednego, where the flames and even the smell of smoke did not touch them. He stands beside you in the lion's den like He did with Daniel, removing the lion's power over you.

Finally, and most significantly, God did not send legions of angels down to wage war on the Roman and Jewish leaders and whisk Jesus away from the terrible suffering of the cross. Jesus went willingly to the cross to save His children from the clutches of the enemy and the consequences of sin, descended into hell to battle against the enemy and bring life from death, and established His Kingdom on earth and in your heart. He delivers you from the ravages of sin, including death, and raises you to eternal life.

Returning to the prior chapter's discussion about your partnership with God, Jesus' protection is all about His partnering with you. Your roles in the partnership are to believe, to trust, and to stand. His roles are to shield your spirit, strengthen you in the midst of the suffering, and redeem.

As part of His protection, Jesus promises redemption. Bad things happen, but you don't have to fear those bad things, knowing "that in all things God works for the good of those who love Him" (Romans 8:28). He "redeems your life from the pit and crowns you with love and compassion" (Psalm 103:4). When the enemy attacks you, Jesus turns the tactics of the enemy back against him. For example, you can learn a lot about yourself by noticing how the enemy chooses to come against you. When the choices of others cause you pain, Jesus comforts you and redeems your suffering, bringing good from it for you.

God does not prevent bad things from happening or cause those bad things to happen. Instead, you have Jesus as your partner, your healing and helping presence, your strength, and your Redeemer in the midst of the bad things that happen. These are the beautiful protections of God.

BELIEVE, TRUST, AND STAND

What is the role of belief in God's protection? It goes back to the part your willingness plays in your relationship with God. Because God gave you free will, you always have a choice. One of the infinite choices you have is whether to believe and accept God's presence in your life. While it is God's desire to be with you, He will never force His will upon you or make you receive what He is offering.

In the book of John alone, Jesus emphasized the importance of belief over 80 times. When you believe, you are given the right to be children of God (John 1:12), you have eternal life (John 3:15), you will not be judged (John 5:24), you will never be thirsty (John 6:35), rivers of living water will flow from within you (John 7:38), you will see the glory of God (John 11:40), you will become children of light (John 12:36) and will not remain in darkness (John 12:46), you will do great works (John 14:12), you will be loved by God (John 16:27), and you are blessed (John 20:29). These are just a few of the powerful promises related to belief.

Paul also talks about the importance of belief. One of the key verses in Scripture is Romans 10:8-10: "The word is near you; it is in your mouth and in your heart, that is, the message concerning faith that we proclaim: If you declare with your mouth, "Jesus is Lord," and believe in your heart that God raised him from the dead, you will be saved. For it is with your heart that you believe and are justified, and it is with your mouth that you profess your faith and are saved." In addition, righteousness is given through faith to those who believe in Jesus (Romans 3:22). Belief also brings freedom (I Corinthians 10:23-24). Your Kingdom inheritance is guaranteed, and His power and strength are given to those who believe (Ephesians 1:18-19).

However, if you don't accept and receive God's presence, He cannot provide these promises. According to James 1:6-8, "you must believe and not doubt, because the one who doubts is like a wave of the sea, blown and tossed by the wind. That person should not expect to receive anything from the Lord. Such a person is double-minded and unstable in all they do." God's decision to partner with you and show you the respect, love, and honor of having a choice means your choice matters. If you choose to reject His presence, He will not be present in you, and everything His presence provides will be lost to you – the peace, joy, assurance, freedom, comfort, healing, power, and strength He gives will not be there for you, not because God doesn't want to provide it, but because He can't, based on your choice.

Beyond believing in Jesus, you are also instructed to trust Him. Trusting is having a firm belief, with confidence and without doubt, in His reliability and His truth. It is possible to believe He is Lord without putting yourself in His hands completely, but to have His protection, you need to place your whole self in His care. Through what He has done for you, He has demonstrated He is good, His love is unfailing, His patience is without end, and His mercy is limitless, proving Himself trustworthy. But trust is a choice, so your role in the partnership is choosing to trust, meaning to rely totally on, who He is and what He has shown you and spoken to you.

The parable of the talents (Matthew 25:14-30) is basically a parable about trust. The first two servants saw the gift of the Master as entrusted (the key word) to them, and they responded by trusting the Master and investing totally. However, the one identified as the wicked, lazy servant believed the Master to be a harsh man. Because he feared the Master and didn't trust his intentions or responses, the wicked servant buried his gift, so it failed to grow. When the Master returned, he took the gift away from the wicked servant and gave it to the good and faithful servant who had done the most with his gift. In the words of the Master in Jesus' tale, "For whoever has will be given more, and they will have an abundance. Whoever does not have, even what they have will be taken from them" (Matthew 25:29).

So, belief is good, but it is not enough. God has trusted you to partner with Him, like the Master in the parable. You must also trust the goodness of the Lord and invest your whole self, totally and completely, in your relationship with Him. You must embrace His truth as absolute and receive it with your whole heart, not burying it under doubts and lies you have believed or allowing it to remain uncultivated and unused. You are to "Trust in the LORD with all your heart and lean not on your own understanding; in all your ways submit to him, and he will make your paths straight" (Proverbs 3:5-6). Like the two servants who trusted their Master, when you invest your whole heart in His presence and truth, "the God of hope will fill you with all joy and peace as you trust in him, so that you may overflow with hope by the power of the Holy Spirit" (Romans 15:13). For whoever has will be given more.

Finally, your role in the protection provided by Jesus is to take a stand against the enemy's schemes. Notice He doesn't ask you to defeat the enemy or to fight him on your own, just to stand firm (Ephesians 6:11-14, I Corinthians 15:58 and 16:13, Philippians 1:27 and 4:1, II Thessalonians 2:15). According to Paul, God makes it possible for you to stand firm by His Spirit (II Corinthians 1:21-22), so as with all things, it isn't up to you alone to take your stand, but by the power of His Spirit you are empowered to stand firm.

II Corinthians 4:7 informs you that you have all-surpassing power, and that this power is from God. When Paul wrote, "We are hard pressed on every side, *but not crushed;* perplexed, *but not in despair;* persecuted, *but not abandoned;* struck down, *but not destroyed"* (II Corinthians 4:8-9), it was God who provided for the preservation and perseverance of his spirit. He went on to say, "Therefore we do not lose heart. Though outwardly we are wasting away, yet inwardly we are being renewed day by day. For our light and momentary troubles are achieving for us an eternal glory that far outweighs them all. So we fix our eyes not on what is seen, but on what is unseen, since what is seen is temporary, but what is unseen is eternal" (II Corinthians 4:16-18).

Paul is describing here the strange phenomenon that is God's protection. From outward appearances, your life may seem no different from anyone else's. You may appear to have the same struggles, the same losses, and the same obstacles to overcome; yet, you experience these hardships differently. Though outwardly you appear "hard-pressed on every side," your spirit is in a continuous state of renewal and restoration. You are strengthened supernaturally in a way unseen by physical eyes, and your eyes are fixed on the unseen.

For most people, their eyes are drawn to the temporal because their physical senses perceive it as reality. What is reality, though? According to these verses, reality is what is unseen, because what is seen is momentary, but what is unseen is everlasting. When you focus your eyes on your circumstances and look for certain outcomes as a measure of God's faithfulness, you will inevitably be knocked off your feet, because the temporal does not reflect the spiritual/eternal reality. You are looking in the wrong place! Your stance must be based on spiritual truth, not worldly evidence. Looking at your circumstances keeps you from moving forward in partnership with God, believing and trusting Him and standing on truth.

As you move through life, enemy attacks can sometimes leave you feeling like a salmon swimming upstream against the current or like a leaf being carried along by the river with no ability to select your destination or correct your course if caught in an eddy, crashed into a rock, or tossed over a waterfall. You might feel like you are out on the ocean far out of the sight of land, running out of fresh water and desperately paddling in some direction in the faint hope that you might get somewhere eventually. At other times, you might feel like you are miles below the surface of the ocean, with no hope of swimming to the surface before you drown, and no air available to you. However, these feelings are not an accurate perception of your state of being.

When you fix your eyes on Jesus, you stand on solid ground. The enemy tries to confuse you with distortions based on past experiences or present circumstances, perverting your view of God's character in order to tempt you to "drink the sea water" (which, as any sailor will tell you, even though it appears wet, will kill you, and kill you quickly). But you have living water always available to you. You have a partner who navigates through rough and opposing waters with you, giving you a solid Rock on which to stand. You have the God-given freedom to choose your own course and to correct your course at any time.

Rather than swimming against or being carried by the current, you are not caught up in the river of life but are standing on the shoreline, outside the physical circumstances, walking purposefully and intentionally in the Kingdom. When you stand in the Kingdom, the physical circumstances lose their power. Your thoughts and feelings align with Jesus, freeing you to make your choices based on truth and separate from temporary outcomes.

You are not desperately paddling the empty ocean alone; you have your Lord who is always with you, ready to transform you and redeem your circumstances, bringing you safely to shore. Instead of drowning under miles of water, you have His truth, which is your air, so that even when your life appears overwhelming or the enemy attempts to thwart you, accuse you, tempt you, and condemn you, which he will, Jesus stands beside you, saying, "Hold onto Me." He carries you up to the surface by breathing His truth into your heart. The truly wonderful news is that all you have to do is turn your eyes to Him and hold on. He does the rest.

SHIELD AND ARMOR

God contends against the enemy on your behalf. In Psalm 35:2-3, David calls on God to "Take up shield and armor; arise and come to my aid. Brandish spear and javelin against those who pursue me." He goes on to say, "Awake and rise to my defense! Contend for me, my God and Lord. Vindicate me in your righteousness" (Psalm 35:23-24).

Who is your enemy? Paul reminds you the battle you fight is "not against flesh and blood, but against the rulers, against the authorities, against the powers of this dark world and against the spiritual forces of evil in the heavenly realms" (Ephesians 6:12). So, when you call, as David did, for the Lord to contend for you, He brings His shield and armor, spear and javelin, against Satan on your behalf.

As a soldier of God, you need to know two basic truths to stand effectively against the enemy. The first truth is God is good. This idea seems very simplistic at first glance, but when you unpack it in its depth you will see it is quite profound.

First, if God is good, there is no evil in Him. "God is light; in him there is no darkness at all" (I John 1:5). Ascribing to God actions of the enemy goes contrary to this Scriptural truth. He doesn't bring bad things on us, nor does He "allow" bad things to happen to us, as if those bad things are His will and serve His

113

purposes. Go back to the earlier chapter about authority and note choices have an impact on the course of life, through Old Testament and New, and in your life as well. Not everything that happens is God's will – far from it. Because God gave freedom to choose, and humankind often chooses evil, God's will is not always done on earth as it is in heaven.

Also, since God is good, God does not share any characteristics with the enemy. God is not prideful, arrogant, condemning, capricious, callous, indifferent, or controlling. Sometimes, the way you hear God described sounds a lot like these traits, but those descriptions are false. These are traits belonging to the enemy, and nothing of the enemy is in God.

God's primary characteristic is deep, abiding love. His love is not the superficial, shallow love of convenience and ease. He doesn't just give you what you want just because you want it; He doesn't provide outcomes to please you or make you happy like an indulgent parent satisfying a spoiled child. Every choice, every action is motivated by an unyielding desire for your good.

His goodness takes the forms of never leaving you, never giving up on you no matter what you do, pursuing you even when you ignore or reject Him, providing for your true needs as you permit, and guiding, helping, and leading you while allowing you freedom to choose that isn't illusory but is real and impactful on your life, on others, and on Him. Yes, God is good. And it is vital that you rightly understand this truth, for without it you will be easily caught up in a fog of confusion and the swirl of the enemy's deception. Without it, you can mistake the heart and nature of God and confuse the enemy's tactics as God's work. From there, Satan can easily build resentment and bitterness toward God, and ultimately rejection of God. Without this cornerstone truth as your anchor, you are adrift.

The second truth you need to know is the enemy's only weapon is the lie. He is "a liar and the father of lies" (John 8:44). Fortunately, he isn't creative. He uses the same lies repeatedly, and the same tactics and strategies, which makes him a predictable adversary, if you pay attention. He uses what is familiar to you against you. So, for example, if you learned as a child that you didn't matter, the enemy will bring that lie against you over and over again, using a variety of methods of delivery, but always the same lie.

If you know God is good, and you know what to expect from Him, then you can rightly identify the enemy's deceptions and place anything of his in his camp. You do not have to internalize Satan's deceptions; in fact, if you refuse to take his lies in, there is nothing he can do about it! Your God-given free will has guaranteed that. Do you see how important your freedom truly is? With it, God provides the mechanism for the ultimate defeat of the enemy.

God provides you with a full set of armor and weapons for you to use in your stand against the enemy. Since Satan only uses lies as his weapon, it makes sense one of your weapons is the truth. Jesus named Himself the way and the truth and the life (John 14:6), so you can see how your best weapon to combat the enemy is His presence within you. Paul called the truth the "belt" around your waist (Ephesians 6:14). The soldier's belt holds the rest of the armor in place, keeping the soldier well-protected. In the same way, His Spirit guides you into all the truth (John 16:13) and keeps you grounded.

115

Proverbs describes the ways the truth of God operates to keep you shielded: "if you accept my words and store up my commands within you, turning your ear to wisdom and applying your heart to understanding—indeed, if you call out for insight and cry aloud for understanding, and if you look for it as for silver and search for it as for hidden treasure...then you will understand what is right and just and fair—every good path. For wisdom will enter your heart, and knowledge will be pleasant to your soul. Discretion will protect you, and understanding will guard you" (Proverbs 2:1-4, 9-11).

Another part of your armor Paul calls "the breastplate of righteousness" (Ephesians 6:14), but it isn't the righteousness of doing good works, something you create in yourself by following God's law. Instead, "righteousness is given through faith in Jesus Christ to all who believe" (Romans 3:22). On your own, you cannot be righteous, but Jesus has made you righteous by cleansing your sins and casting them far away from you. Because of your faith in Jesus, you no longer have to feel the torturous pain of shame, which acts as quicksand, sucking you deeper into sin. "Therefore, there is now no condemnation for those who are in Christ Jesus, because through Christ Jesus the law of the Spirit who gives life has set you free from the law of sin and death" (Romans 8:1-2). The breastplate protects your heart from the crushing devastation of condemnation for your sin; instead, your sins are forgiven, and you are set free. Jesus Himself becomes your righteousness (I Corinthians 1:30).

Living in accordance with the truth means you are, "with regard to your former way of life, to put off your old self, which is being corrupted by its deceitful desires; to be made new in the attitude of your minds; and to put on the new self, created to be like

God in true righteousness and holiness" (Ephesians 4:22-24). Do you see how the belt and the breastplate work together? Your breastplate is effective when it remains in place, aligned properly, stable and secure. You no longer desire the ways of the flesh. The truth brings healing relief. Living in His truth feels infinitely better than slavery to sin, because freedom feels better than bondage. As is the case with all your armor, only the Lord can provide your breastplate and secure it with His truth.

The next aspect of your armor has multiple parts. The first element is the good news, or the gospel. According to Paul, the gospel on which you take your stand (I Corinthians 15:1), which is of first importance (I Corinthians 15:3) is as follows: "Christ died for our sins, according to the Scriptures, that he was buried, that he was raised on the third day according to the Scriptures" (I Corinthians 15:3-4). Everything hinges on this good news. Nothing else matters if you do not know the source of your salvation.

The firm foundation of the gospel gives authority, certainty, and strength to your ability to stand. You are then ready for whatever comes. Additionally, you have the peace provided by your assurance that Christ has taken care of your sins through His death, and He has overcome death for you through His resurrection. All fears are rooted in the fundamental fear of death that human beings share; however, Christ has taken away the need for that basic fear, undercutting the foundation of all other fears. Remember, "perfect love drives out fear" (I John 4:18), and since Jesus demonstrated His perfect love on the cross, fear has no more ground to stand on in you when you stand on the gospel.

Paul goes on to instruct you to take up the shield of faith. Earlier in this chapter, I talked about belief as an important element of God's protection. When you connect belief (being fully persuaded of something) with trust (having confidence without doubt) with response or action based on what you believe and trust, you have faith.

You can begin to see how each element of the armor builds one upon the other. You begin with truth, which holds everything together. Truth is coupled with the righteousness that comes from belief in Jesus. You are readied to stand in peace by confidence in the gospel (trust). Now you take action ("take up"), based on the truth which you believe and trust and stand upon (faith), using your shield to extinguish the arrows of the enemy. "For in the gospel the righteousness of God is revealed—a righteousness that is by faith from first to last, just as it is written: 'The righteous will live by faith'" (Romans 1:17).

How does faith deflect attacks from the enemy? Faith in Scripture is called "confidence in what we hope for and assurance about what we do not see" (Hebrews 11:1). The writer of Hebrews goes on the describe the many actions of faith from the Old Testament, from Abel to Enoch to Noah to Abraham to Isaac to Jacob to Joseph to Moses to Joshua to Rahab to David and so on, as examples of what faith looks like for believers to follow. These individuals believed God, trusted Him, and followed His leading, even when God's direction didn't make sense to them or placed them in danger. Since the arrows of the enemy are all lies, and faith is certainty of the truth and the confidence to act even if the reason is unseen, and truth undergirds faith, the enemy's lies cannot find purchase. The depth of your assurance repels them. You bring your faith (belief + trust + action) to bear against the enemy's arrows, making them unable to penetrate the truth.

118

The key to your shield's effectiveness is that all-in confidence that defines faith. Wielding your faith tentatively or buying into uncertainty leaves you partially exposed. Imagine the enemy standing across from you, raising his bow to shoot an arrow toward you. If you are "all-in," you would immediately raise your shield with confidence, trusting God will deflect the arrow, relying on His truth to be absolute and certain. However, if you are plagued with questioning and doubt, you might take the time to consider running away or even surrendering to the enemy out of fear, and by the time you hesitantly lift your shield, the arrow has already found the crack in your armor and found purchase. Then the enemy accuses God of failing in His protection, and you are likely to agree, further undermining your faith.

Consider Peter, who said to Jesus, "tell me to come to you on the water," and when Jesus said, "Come," Peter walked on the water toward Jesus without difficulty. But when he noticed the wind (the physical realm), he doubted Jesus. I imagine his thoughts were something like, "What am I doing? I can't walk on top of water! I'm going to drown out here!" Fear seized Peter, so he started to sink. What happened next? "Immediately Jesus reached out his hand and caught him. 'You of little faith,' he said, 'why did you doubt?'" (Matthew 14:28-31). Jesus' statement to Peter makes it clear why he sank. Doubt undermined his faith, and the enemy's arrow pierced him. Jesus didn't fail to protect Peter; in fact, despite Peter's doubt, Jesus reached out to him and lifted him up. Peter's doubt was the reason he sank at all.

The next elements of your armor complete your covering. Once again, you can see how the whole armor works together. Paul described it this way: "And you also were included in Christ when

119

you heard the message of truth, the gospel of your salvation. When you believed, you were marked in him with a seal, the promised Holy Spirit, who is a deposit guaranteeing our inheritance until the redemption of those who are God's possession—to the praise of his glory" (Ephesians 1:13-14). You receive the truth, the gospel, which brings salvation to those who believe. Your salvation is a covering over you, a protection for your thoughts from fear, sealed by the Holy Spirit in you and guaranteed by His presence. This same Spirit provides you with a sword for battle, a sword made from the words of God He writes in your heart and mind. As Scripture says, "the word of God lives in you, and you have overcome the evil one" (I John 2:14). You wield the sword against the enemy by fighting lies with His truth. And with that, you have come full circle, back to the belt of truth that holds everything in place.

Paul's final instruction for warfare is to "pray in the Spirit on all occasions" (Ephesians 6:18). Often overlooked in the description of God's armor, prayer is the most important element. You need to talk with Jesus, on a continuous basis, to receive the applicable truth needed to combat the enemy in each moment. In addition, you can receive His assurance, have Him bolster your faith with His power, have Him help you keep your eyes fixed on the unseen and not get caught up in the worldly realm, discern the presence of the enemy, see others through His eyes to change your perception to one of love, and hear His warnings, all of which are His provisions for your protection.

REDEMPTION

I started this chapter with a discussion on the difference between prevention and protection. This key difference is a stumbling block for many in their relationship with God, because they are looking for prevention of bad things happening to them instead of seeking God's redemption of those difficulties and struggles. However, if you read the Bible, you'll see the whole of Scripture is a story of redemption. Indeed, every major player has a redemption story of their own. So do you.

I won't watch a movie or read a book that ends without redemption as part of the story, but those wonderful stories where it appears all is lost, where the hero or heroine stands to lose everything but continues to stand, those are the stories I love and will watch or read over and over again. I love those stories because they are a reflection of the story of God in relationship with us.

Most of Jesus' followers suffered greatly after His resurrection, but their eyes weren't fixed on their circumstances. Stephen's story is one of my favorites (Acts 6 & 7). Stephen, filled with the Holy Spirit, was preaching with such wisdom that those who tried to oppose what he was saying found they couldn't argue effectively against him. Instead, they brought false witnesses against him before the Sanhedrin. But Stephen didn't cower in fear; instead, he challenged them openly with truth. When the Jewish leaders threatened him, all Stephen saw was Jesus standing at the right hand of God. It was as if the world faded from his eyes, and he was consumed with the Kingdom of God. While the Jewish leaders stoned him, Stephen asked Jesus not to hold their sin against them, then he fell asleep. Do you see Jesus' protection and redemption in this beautiful story? Yes, being stoned to death was a horrific way to die. It sometimes took days of pummeling before you passed. But here is Stephen, praying for his abusers and focusing his eyes on Jesus, falling asleep as the rain of stones fell on his head. Again,

God didn't prevent the stoning. He didn't 'fix' it for Stephen – not in the worldly sense. But the redemption is far superior to any temporary 'fix' you might have expected.

I also love the story of Peter's imprisonment in Acts 12. Herod arrested Peter and planned to put him to death after Passover, but God had other plans. "The night before Herod was to bring him to trial, Peter was sleeping between two soldiers, bound with two chains, and sentries stood guard at the entrance. Suddenly an angel of the Lord appeared, and a light shone in the cell. He struck Peter on the side and woke him up. "Quick, get up!" he said, and the chains fell off Peter's wrists. Then the angel said to him, "Put on your clothes and sandals." And Peter did so. "Wrap your cloak around you and follow me," the angel told him. Peter followed him out of the prison, but he had no idea that what the angel was doing was really happening; he thought he was seeing a vision" (Acts 12:6-9). What strikes me most about this story is Peter's response to being imprisoned and facing death. The angel had to wake him up from a deep sleep – so sound was Peter sleeping, so deep was his peace, the angel had to strike him to wake him, and Peter thought he was still dreaming, not realizing he was really being freed until after the angel left him. Peter wasn't worried about his fate. He didn't fear Herod or death. Like Stephen, he had his eyes fixed on Jesus, and God's peace beyond understanding consumed him.

Another favorite redemption story of mine is the story of Paul and Silas in prison (Acts 16:16-40). Paul and Silas were stripped and beaten severely, then bound in chains in an inner cell. What was their response? They sang hymns to God with the other prisoners listening in. A violent earthquake caused all the doors of the prison to swing open and all the prisoners' chains to fall off. The jailer, knowing what would happen to him if his prisoners escaped, readied to kill himself, but Paul called to him to stop, saying, "We are all here!" As a result, the jailer asked Paul how he could be saved. Paul and Silas spoke to the jailer, then to his whole household, and all were saved. The jailer washed their wounds and fed them, and the next day, the magistrates, learning Paul and Silas were Roman citizens, released them. Paul and Silas, filled with peace and joy in the midst of their imprisonment, praying and singing hymns for all the prisoners, also experienced the great joy of bringing an entire household to God, and perhaps some of the other prisoners as well. What a wonderful redemption of a horrible experience!

I believe you notice what you seek. For example, if you are looking for shapes of animals in the clouds, you're likely to find a bunny or a dragon. If you are looking for beauty on walks in nature, you'll notice the beauty, but if you watch for snakes and bugs, you'll miss the beauty and will see every creepy crawly thing along your path. The same is true of God's redemption. If your eyes are consumed by your circumstances, you may miss God's beautiful redemption of those circumstances in your story. But, if like Stephen, Peter, Paul, and Silas, your eyes are fixed on Jesus during your difficult circumstances, you will find unexplainable peace, even joy, as He walks with you through the difficulty and turns it for good for you and others, bringing redemption out of the suffering.

CONCLUSION

Jesus promises protection for His children, but His protection doesn't take the form of preventing bad things, which would interfere with your freedom to choose and others' choices as well. No, Jesus loves you too much to take away your freedom. Instead, He offers His presence to bring peace, comfort, warmth, joy, and hope, He provides armor that shields your spirit from the ravages of the enemy's assaults, and He provides redemption, bringing good out of your terrible circumstances and healing for your heart from the pain those circumstances cause. His protection relies on your partnership with Him, including your roles of choosing to believe Him, trusting Him, and standing in faith.

His Spirit surrounds you and shields you, like the fire and cloud that surrounded Israel and marched them out of Egypt's clutches and into the land of promise. Under His protection, you are:

Free to believe Jesus' promises and rely on His presence to meet your needs;

Free to see God's redemption of your circumstances, even in difficult times;

Free from doubts about God's goodness and His love for you;

Free to trust God operationalize this trust through standing in faith;

Free from focusing on the physical world, fixing your eyes instead on Jesus and walking in His Kingdom;

Free to set your own course in life rather than being swept along in life's current;

Free to partner with Jesus and rely on His Spirit and truth within your heart to deflect the enemy's arrows.

Peace comes from knowing, no matter your circumstances, your Redeemer lives within you and will take what the world brings your way and turn it for good. Joy comes from doubt evaporating in the experience of His presence, the reception of His truth, and the protection He provides. His protection, and the freedom that accompanies it, are like shining gems surrounding you on your journey through life toward your own promised land.

STARTING POINT: QUESTIONS TO EXPLORE HIS PROTECTION

Answer the following questions to further explore the protection God provides. Consider your answers prayerfully and thoughtfully. Don't offer a superficial response and move on to the next question but look deeply within and be as honest with yourself as you can be. Avoid giving "pat" answers you might have heard in church, particularly if you've not examined what those responses mean in depth. These questions are designed to help you understand and experience His protection and learn to see His redemption.

1. In what ways have you experienced the protection of God in your life?
2. What are some situations where you questioned God's goodness or assumed He did not protect you?
3. What role do you see your belief playing in how God protects you?
4. How would you describe the difference between belief, trust, and faith?
5. Where in your life do you need to renew your stand against the enemy?
6. How has God's truth been armor for your spirit?

7. What are some examples of truth you have been fully
   persuaded of and are confident in?
8. How has the full armor of God protected you from the evil
   one? Where has your armor been hindered by doubt?
9. In what ways are you like Peter walking on the water? In
   what ways are you like Stephen?
10. What are some examples of God's redemption in your life?

Destination: Prayers to access His Protection

Find a quiet place with few distractions to sit with Jesus.
Still your mind and quiet your heart by repeating a verse of
Scripture meaningful to you; for example, you could repeat,
"my God is my rock, in whom I take refuge, my shield and the horn
of my salvation" (Psalm 18:2). I have written a prayer for you as an
example, but use your own words, from your heart, to ask Jesus to
reveal His protection: *Lord, you are a loving God, and I know you
are good, but sometimes the enemy tries to say that because bad
things still happen, you aren't good and you aren't protecting me. I
would like to see your goodness and understand how and why bad
things happen sometimes. Would you show me and help me
experience your goodness? And would you help me to see the role
choices and the hand of the enemy play in bad circumstances?*
After you pray, spend time in silent meditation, eyes closed
and listening for His answers. He may show you an image in your
mind, or you may hear words or phrases in your mind, or you may
sense emotions or experiences He brings to you to reveal His
goodness. He might bring to mind a particular verse or story from
Scripture that reveals some aspect of His protection. You can

recognize responses from the Lord by the peace they stir up in your heart. If an image or word comes to you that brings anxiety or shame, reject it, recenter yourself on Jesus, and ask again. If you think you hear a response that contradicts Scripture, pray against enemy interference, recenter on Jesus, and ask again. Otherwise, don't analyze what comes up or question if it's the Lord. Instead, go with it and follow wherever He takes you. If you are getting "off base," He will let you know. Keep with it, asking Jesus to explain anything you don't understand and to show you more, until you feel He is finished.

If you don't hear anything, don't be concerned or frustrated. Remember, we have an enemy who actively opposes our treasure seeking and tries to thwart our relationship with Jesus. Take a break and come back to your prayer later. This time, if you don't receive a response, ask Jesus what is in the way. It may be a lie you believe, such as God doesn't care about you or God has some other agenda that is more important to Him than you are, or it may be distractions of life the enemy is using to get in your way. False beliefs about God can also hinder making a connection; for example, seeing God as uninvolved, distant, and indifferent. Whatever Jesus reveals is in the way, ask Him to bring truth to your heart to move the hindrance out of your way. Then return to your prayer request.

Another prayer you could pursue is asking Jesus to strengthen your faith. For example, you could pray: *Lord, I believe what you say is true, and I want to trust you and stand on your truth. Sometimes, though, doubt starts to rise up in me. I don't want to doubt, but it still comes. I'm like the man who said Lord I believe, help my unbelief. I want to be like Peter when he stepped out of the boat, not like Peter when he noticed the wind. Would you please help to strengthen my faith so I can stand firm?* Listen for His suggestions on how to stand against the enemy. Check with Him on areas where you are still trying to handle things on your own instead of relying on His partnership. Remember that truth is absolute and unchanging, just as He is the same always.

Another area for prayer involves spiritual warfare and the use of His armor. An example of this type of prayer could be: *Lord, I choose to put on your full armor. Bring truth to my heart and mind to hold everything in place. Establish me in your righteousness through faith and cover my heart. Remind me of the firm foundation on which I stand so I am ready and at peace in my spirit. Be my shield and my sword against the evil one. Cover me with your presence. Go before me like the fire and cloud. Would you please help me to rely on you and you alone for all my needs?* As you pray, Jesus may bring to mind lies you are believing, or He may point out hindrances to your ability to extinguish the enemy's arrows. When He shows you these things, ask Him for the truth you need to remove the lies. Seek to understand where doubt is interfering with your shield and ask for help with those doubts.

Finally, you could pray for Jesus' help in opening your eyes to see His redemption. Your prayer could be: *Lord, you are my Redeemer. I am going through this difficult time in my life, and I'm struggling to see any good in it or coming from it. Would you please open my eyes to see and understand your redemption of these circumstances?* Jesus might help you to take five steps back from your situation to see it from a different perspective. Seeking His presence in the circumstance may open your heart to receive His peace, so you become more like Stephen in seeing only the

Kingdom truth. He may bring patience to your heart to continue to wait and watch for His redemption to come.

As a partner with Jesus and participant in your protection, your choices, your beliefs, and your actions play an important role; however, always remember you are not in this life alone. You are not a leaf floating along in a river. You are not adrift alone in a boat far from shore. You are not miles below the surface of the ocean, ill-equipped and drowning. Your salvation, your righteousness, your faith, your hope, and your solid ground of truth are with you always, no matter your circumstances, for Jesus is all those for you. His presence is your certainty and your assurance.

SETTING THE COURSE: LIVING IN HIS PROTECTION

The first section presents concepts you may want to internalize, and the second section lists some actions you may take to apply the information you have studied. Approach the following concepts and actions prayerfully. Avoid any thinking that you must rigidly adhere to them, because these are only suggestions and may not work for you. Everyone is different. Remember, your faith isn't up to you alone but is established through His presence and power combined with your choice to believe. Use these suggestions to deepen your reliance on Him in your quest to live the Kingdom life.

INTERNALIZE THE CONCEPTS

Consider the implications of God's protection vs. His prevention. Meditate on the ways His presence impacts your perception of your circumstances.

Examine how partnership with Jesus affects His protection. Consider your roles in the partnership and compare them with His roles in the partnership.

Contemplate the goodness of God. Consider evidence in Scripture and in your own life of His goodness. Examine the differences between God and the enemy. Meditate on the truth that nothing is in common between them.

Consider the advantages of establishing and choosing your own course for life as opposed to being carried along my circumstances. Contemplate what it means to stand on God's solid ground as opposed to being swept along in the river of life. Meditate on the meaning of God's truth providing air for you when you are under the deep waters of life.

Consider how all elements of the armor of God work in concert to provide a full covering for you. Contemplate each aspect of your armor and consider how each one serves to protect you.

Examine the examples of faith described in Scripture. Evaluate which elements appear to strengthen faith, enabling the individual to stand firm. Consider Peter's thoughts as he stepped out onto the water as opposed to his thoughts when he noticed the wind and began to sink.

Contemplate the many faces of God's redemption. Meditate on the role of God's presence in establishing peace and joy despite difficult circumstances. Consider the impact of your focus on whether you notice God's redemption or miss seeing it.

PROCESS THEIR APPLICATION

Affirm the goodness of God by keeping a list of examples of His goodness in your life. These items can be answered prayers, unexpected blessings, healing of wounds in your heart, things you are grateful for, and experiences of His love for you. Stay away from focusing on physical realities. For example, when looking for blessings, don't focus on such things as money or position; instead, center your attention on spiritual blessings and things that matter in the Kingdom. When looking for healing, don't focus only on the body, which for everyone is eventually doomed to fail; instead, focus on the spirit, where His healing is eternal.

When you feel lost or adrift, remind yourself of your ability to choose your own course by listing your choices aloud. Be intentional in choosing. Evaluate whether you are being influenced in your choices by fear, and if you are, stop and list all your choices again, then choose from the ones that fear did not influence.

Keep a journal of truth you have learned from Jesus. These truths can be things you have received from Jesus in prayer, things you have learned from studying Scripture, or words of wisdom received from others that you confirmed with Scripture. Do not accept as truth anything heard from someone else without checking with Jesus first in prayer to determine if the truth is accurate and valid. Read over the truths you have recorded on a consistent basis to remind yourself of those truths, so you can pull them up when they are needed to stand against an enemy attack. When doubt plagues your thoughts, review your truth journal, choose a relevant truth, and meditate on that truth until you feel your peace reestablished. Make a commitment to Him to go "all-in" with Him, choosing to trust His truth and relying on His help to fulfill your commitment.

Start your day by putting on your armor with Jesus in prayer, checking with Him that everything is in place. Then, throughout the day, check in, using the weapon of prayer to ask Jesus the state of your armor.

Begin to look for God's redemption during and following difficult circumstances. Be intentional and persistent in seeking to see where His redemption will show up. If His redemption has not already been made evident, assume it will come, keep watch for it, and ask Jesus in prayer to reveal it to you.

The most important thing for you to choose is to let go of self-protection. When you choose to protect yourself, you take God's place, not leaving room for His protection to engulf you. Recognize and accept the failure of your self-protection by honestly evaluating its effectiveness. When you build walls against others, do those walls actually keep you safe, or are you just as hurt when someone rejects you? Do your walls protect you, or do they imprison you? Look at the choices you have made based on fear, and see if the results of those choices turned out as you hoped, or did they create what you most feared? Once you evaluate the lack of efficacy of self-protection, you will want to go to God in humility and ask Him to reestablish His protection in all its forms.

FIVE

The Treasure of Sanctification

YOUR COMPASS

They are not of the world, even as I am not of it. Sanctify them by the truth; your word is truth. As you sent me into the world, I have sent them into the world (John 17:16-18).

He does not treat us as our sins deserve or repay us according to our iniquities. For as high as the heavens are above the earth, so great is his love for those who fear him; as far as the east is from the west, so far has he removed our transgressions from us (Psalm 103:10-12).

May God himself, the God of peace, sanctify you through and through. May your whole spirit, soul and body be kept blameless at the coming of our Lord Jesus Christ. The one who calls you is faithful, and he will do it (I Thessalonians 5:23-24).

He entered the Most Holy Place once for all by his own blood, thus obtaining eternal redemption. The blood of goats and bulls and the ashes of a heifer sprinkled on those who are ceremonially unclean sanctify them, so that they are outwardly clean. How much more, then, will the blood of Christ, who through the eternal Spirit offered himself unblemished to God, cleanse our consciences from acts that lead to death, so that we may serve the living God! For this reason, Christ is the mediator of a new covenant, that those who are called may receive the promised eternal inheritance—now that he has died as a ransom to set them free from the sins committed under the first covenant. You have come to God, the Judge of all, to the spirits of the righteous made perfect, to Jesus the mediator of a new covenant (Hebrews 9:12-15; 12:23-24).

Your faith is growing more and more, and the love all of you have for one another is increasing. All this is evidence that God's judgment is right, and as a result you will be counted worthy of the kingdom of God, for which you are suffering. God is just: He will pay back trouble to those who trouble you and give relief to you who are troubled, and to us as well (II Thessalonians 1:3, 5-7).

You, therefore, have no excuse, you who pass judgment on someone else, for at whatever point you judge another, you are condemning yourself, because you who pass judgment do the same things. Now we know that God's judgment against those who do such things is based on truth. So when you, a mere human being, pass judgment on them and yet do the same things, do you think you will escape God's judgment? Or do you show contempt for the riches of his kindness, forbearance and patience, not realizing that God's kindness is intended to lead you to repentance? (Romans 2:1-4).

I have fought the good fight, I have finished the race, I have kept the faith. Now there is in store for me the crown of righteousness, which the Lord, the righteous Judge, will award to me on that day—and not only to me, but also to all who have longed for his appearing (II Timothy 4:7-8).

Very truly I tell you, whoever hears my word and believes him who sent me has eternal life and will not be judged but has crossed over from death to life (John 5:24).

Who are you to judge someone else's servant? To their own master, servants stand or fall. And they will stand, for the Lord is able to make them stand. For we will all stand before God's judgment seat…each of us will give an account of ourselves to God (Romans 14:4, 10, 12).

MAP KEY: EVIDENTIARY EXCLUSION

SANCTIFICATION DEFINED

*J*esus has made you holy.

'Whoa, wait a minute,' you are probably saying. 'I am anything but holy.' Yet, Scripture is clear the blood of Jesus has cleansed you, washed you through and through, freed you from sin, and made you "whiter than snow" (Psalm 51:7).

Jesus prayed for the Father to sanctify those He sends into the world who are not of the world, those who belong to Him (John 17:16-18). So, what was He asking God to do? To sanctify means to set apart and declare as holy, to consecrate as sacred and dedicated to God, to purify and cleanse free from sin, to approve, and to exculpate or declare not guilty of wrongdoing. This is what Jesus asked for on your behalf, and this is what He accomplished on the cross.

Without Jesus, shame is a thick, black, impenetrable cloak that covers you, in which you hide your face from God and from your true self. When Adam and Eve ate of the knowledge of good and evil, their first response was to cover themselves because of their shame. Since that beginning, the presence of sin has resulted in shame, and since "all have sinned and fall short of the glory of God" (Romans 3:23), all are covered in shame. Because of the cross, the shedding of His blood as the once-and-for-all eternal redemption, when you hear His word and believe (John 5:24), Jesus lifts the cloak of shame off you, making it possible for you to stand before the throne of God without judgment (John 5:24).

How do you imagine it will be when you stand before the throne of God in the Kingdom of Heaven? All will give an account, Scripture tells us (Matthew 12:36, Romans 14:12, Hebrews 4:13, I Peter 4:5) and everything will be laid bare. So, do you imagine yourself standing before God with eyes downcast, while your sins are paraded one by one before all? Do you believe you will approach God's throne with fear and shame?

How does this view line up with the prophesies of Isaiah and Jeremiah, who both state God will no longer remember our sins (Isaiah 43:25; Jeremiah 31:33-34), or Psalm 103:12, which states, "as far as the east is from the west, so far has he removed our transgressions from us"? Hebrews 4:16 says, "Let us then approach God's throne of grace with confidence, so that we may receive mercy and find grace to help us in our time of need." Approaching the throne with confidence does not sound much like an image of trembling in fear and shame as your sins are paraded before your eyes.

No, through Christ, you are sanctified. You stand before God's throne, holy and pure, sinless and without blemish or defect, made so by the blood of Jesus, the Lamb of God. As I Peter 1:3-5, 18-19 explains: "Praise be to the God and Father of our Lord Jesus Christ! In his great mercy he has given us new birth into a living hope through the resurrection of Jesus Christ from the dead, and into an inheritance that can never perish, spoil or fade. This inheritance is kept in heaven for you, who through faith are shielded by God's power until the coming of the salvation that is ready to be revealed in the last time. For you know that it was not with perishable things such as silver or gold that you were redeemed from the empty way of life handed down to you from your ancestors, but with the precious blood of Christ, a lamb without blemish or defect."

Only one question matters before God's throne: did you receive Jesus as Lord of your life and your savior? Did you accept His blood payment of the ransom to free you from the debt caused by sin? If the answer is yes, God sees you as He sees Jesus, holy and blameless, sinless and pure. You are judged by His blood alone. If, however, the answer is no, you must give account for your own actions and make payment for your sin yourself. It is not God's will that one would be lost, but His profound love for you allows you to make your own choice. Still, He pursues you your entire life, offering Himself to you, planting seeds of truth, providing opportunities, whispering love to your heart, and reaching His hand out to you.

Although Jesus has always been with you, you were not always aware of His presence or open to receive Him. The cloak of shame covered your eyes and muted your ears. Because of your shame, you hid yourself from God. Jesus explained to His disciples that this was the reason He spoke in parables: "Though seeing, they do not see; though hearing, they do not hear or understand. In them is fulfilled the prophecy of Isaiah: 'You will be ever hearing but never understanding; you will be ever seeing but never perceiving. For this people's heart has become calloused; they hardly hear with their ears, and they have closed their eyes. Otherwise they might see with their eyes, hear with their ears, understand with their hearts and turn, and I would heal them.' But blessed are your eyes because they see, and your ears because they hear" (Matthew 13:13-16).

The cloak of shame also disconnected you from your true self. You saw yourself through the blackened lens of the shame covering and judged yourself unworthy, unloved, unwanted, and unredeemable. But Jesus only sees you through the eyes of truth. He knows the true nature He created within you. Though that nature is covered with shame to your eyes, in His eyes you have always been the beautiful heart He created, destined for eternity with Him (Ecclesiastes 3:11). Throughout your life, He has called to you, "Arise, my darling, my beautiful one, come with me" (Song of Songs 2:10). Despite what you believe when you see yourself through the lens of shame, Jesus has always said to you, "You are altogether beautiful, my darling; there is no flaw in you" (Song of Songs 4:7).

138

I John 4:17 says, "This is how love is made complete among us so that we will have confidence on the day of judgment: In this world we are like Jesus." What an outlandish idea! We are like Jesus? Yet, that is exactly what Isaiah prophesied would happen when Messiah came: "Though your sins are like scarlet, they shall be as white as snow; though they are red as crimson, they shall be like wool" (Isaiah 1:18). He is the Lamb without blemish, and He makes you like Him.

BEFORE THE JUDGE

Every moment of every day, Satan, the accuser (Revelation 12:10) stands before the judge and brings charges against you. As your prosecutor, he indicts you with wrongdoing and presents evidence of your misconduct, stacking that evidence against you in ever-rising mounds. He is always ready to pull out old evidence of your past deeds to justify and corroborate his current accusations. He divides the evidence into categories (proof you are unworthy of love, proof everything is your fault, proof you want to be in control, proof you are selfish and self-centered, proof you don't measure up, proof of malicious intent, and on and on), ready to dump the whole load of similar examples at your feet with each misstep. He is always mounting his case against you. Can you see his evidence boxes, neatly labeled, stacked high to the ceiling in the evidence room, with your name on them?

But, the trick of the enemy is he doesn't present his case before the Righteous Judge. If he did, the Judge would find for the defendant. No, Satan presents his accusations to you. You sit on the judgment seat over yourself. You are both defendant and judge in your case, and when presented with the evidence, you find the defendant guilty. Your verdict against yourself feeds the shame cloak, which separates you farther from the One who would come to your defense. So, the trial is fixed.

Thankfully, the trial is also a sham. God is righteous and will not allow a miscarriage of justice to stand, so He sends Jesus to your defense and takes your place on the judgment seat as the True Judge. When the enemy opens the evidence room door and trots out his boxes upon boxes of evidence, Jesus argues on your behalf, based on your acceptance of His actions on the cross in exchange for your debt, and the Judge excludes the evidence against you. All of Satan's so-called evidence is thrown out, because it was illegally obtained. You see, the righteous requirements of the law have been fulfilled (Romans 8:4), and you have "died to the law through the body of Christ" (Romans 7:4). You have been set free from what once bound you and released from the law, so you are free to "serve in the new way of the Spirit, and not in the old way of the written code" (Romans 7:6).

"Therefore, there is now no condemnation for those who are in Christ Jesus, because through Christ Jesus the law of the Spirit who gives life has set you free from the law of sin and death" (Romans 8:1-2). Satan's accusations are based on the old way, the law of sin and death, which no longer stands. Interestingly enough, Satan is quite a fan of the law, because through the law you become conscious of your sin (Romans 3:20), you are charged with your sin (Romans 5:13), and sin increases (Romans 5:20). Ever opportunistic, Satan uses the law to craft his accusations, even though, thanks be to Jesus, "You are not under the law but under grace" (Romans 6:14). Thus, the evidence against you has been

140

illicitly obtained and must be excluded. The trumped-up case against you is thrown out because of a complete lack of evidence.

You might say, 'Then, why not sin more?' This argument was the same one Paul refuted in his letters (Romans 3:8, Romans 6:1-2, 6:15, Galatians 2:17, I Corinthians 6:12, 10:13). Once Christ lives in your heart and becomes the cornerstone of your life, your desire begins to mirror His. This transformation is part of His treasure of sanctification. This doesn't mean you never sin again, for, as Paul says, "I have the *desire* to do what is good, but I cannot carry it out. For I do not do the good I want to do, but the evil I do not want to do—this I keep on doing" (Romans 7:18-19); however, he goes on to say, "Who will rescue me from this body that is subject to death? Thanks be to God, who delivers me through Jesus Christ our Lord!" (Romans 7:24-25). What changes in you through your sanctification is your heart's desire.

So, the ruling has already been made on the accusations of the enemy and his evidence against you. The evidence has been excluded, and you have been found not guilty, by reason of the blood of Christ. You can shed the cloak of shame once and for all and walk in the light of the certain knowledge of God's love and acceptance. You can walk out of that courtroom, free from the chains of sin, for you are holy and blameless. You are sanctified.

MATURITY

Just as child development goes through different stages, from developing trust to gaining autonomy to taking initiative and responsibility to accomplishment to discovering identity, faith also has a developmental arc. Faith generally begins with a concrete, literal understanding. What you are taught by an authority is often

141

accepted without question. As faith progresses, you adopt a legalistic view, with very black-and-white thinking. You continue to conform to authority but begin to develop a personal faith, as long as your beliefs don't conflict with the authority's beliefs. Then, a growing faith develops openness to complexities and takes responsibility for your own beliefs. Questioning your understanding may cause a crisis of faith, but as faith continues to develop, conflicts in belief are resolved, and the deeper meanings in metaphor and symbolism are understood. Finally, you reach maturity in your faith, holding onto universal principles to guide your understanding, such as love, righteousness, and justice, and making your choices based on those guiding, underlying principles.

Looking at Paul's writings on the law, sin, and grace, you can begin to see his arguments for mature faith, one guided by the truths of Christ and principles of love and justice, as opposed to following the law under authority or under social pressure. In other words, Paul is describing what it is like to have spiritual maturity. You follow the path of Christ, not because you have to but because you want to; not because He said so but because you love Him and desire to align with Him and the values and principles He espouses. You begin to see as He sees.

You are no longer bound to the law, because you no longer need the law to direct your choices. If you have no desire to kill, you don't need a law to keep you from committing murder. If you desire to make choices from a heart of love, commands saying don't steal, don't covet, don't lie, etc., are unnecessary, because you don't desire to cause others harm. Love for God and oneness with the Holy Spirit living within guides your choices.

As Jesus said, all the law and prophets are contained in the commandment to love God and love your neighbor (Matthew 22:36-40). Jesus gave the disciples a new commandment: to love one another (John 13:34), and Paul reiterated, "For the entire law is fulfilled in keeping this one command: "Love your neighbor as yourself" (Galatians 5:14), and "Let no debt remain outstanding, except the continuing debt to love one another, for whoever loves others has fulfilled the law. The commandments, 'You shall not commit adultery,' 'You shall not murder,' 'You shall not steal,' 'You shall not covet,' and whatever other command there may be, are summed up in this one command: 'Love your neighbor as yourself.' Love does no harm to a neighbor. Therefore, love is the fulfillment of the law" (Romans 13:8-10). Therefore, all that remains to follow is love.

So, the law fulfilled its purpose by revealing your sin and showing you that you can't be righteous by your own efforts, "for if righteousness could be gained through the law, Christ died for nothing!" (Galatians 2:21). The law let you know you need Jesus, and now that you have Jesus, you no longer need the law to instruct you what to do.

Paul warns of the dangers of binding yourself once more to the law. Having been set free to live by the Spirit, you don't want to go back under the "yoke of slavery" (Galatians 5:1), to either the law or to sin. According to Paul, if you bind yourself back to even one law, you become obligated to the whole law, because you are not accepting God's grace. Paul's description of the consequences of this obligation to the law is harsh: "You who are trying to be justified by the law have been *alienated* from Christ; you have fallen away from grace" (Galatians 5:4). In other words, in walking

143

away from grace, you put yourself back in the position of justifying your own actions before the throne of God.

Scripture challenges those who lack spiritual maturity to move beyond the elementary teachings about Christ and become acquainted with true righteousness, wisdom, and through constant practice, discerning good from evil (Hebrews 5:12-14, 6:1). Also, you are encouraged to embrace trials and tests of faith to strengthen your perseverance, "so that you may be mature and complete, not lacking anything" (James 1:2-4). Paul describes maturity as "attaining to the whole measure of the fullness of Christ," and goes on to say, "Then we will no longer be infants, tossed back and forth by the waves, and blown here and there by every wind of teaching and by the cunning and craftiness of people in their deceitful scheming. Instead, speaking the truth in love, we will grow to become in every respect the mature body of him who is the head, that is, Christ" (Ephesians 4:13-15). To reach maturity, he says you must "be made new in the attitude of your minds; and to put on the new self, created to be like God in true righteousness and holiness" (Ephesians 4:23-24).

The spiritually mature have also moved past a focus on worldly things (I Corinthians 3:1-3). Circumstances no longer dictate your feelings and beliefs. You don't gather your evidence from the physical world to tell you who God is or to determine your faith in Him. Instead, your evidence is your own experience of His presence. You know the unseen Kingdom is reality because you have personally experienced its power.

How does a toddler learn to walk, or a child to swim? Their loving parent stands before them, hands outstretched, saying, "Come to me." The child doesn't trust the water to catch him; the baby doesn't believe in the ground to hold her up. Out of love and trust in the parent, the baby takes its first step, and the child jumps into the pool. If they looked at the circumstances, they would never move and learn. In the same way, you walk forward out of love for and trust in God, and your faith (belief+trust+action) helps you persevere and endure as you learn and grow.

As you grow in spiritual maturity, you begin to see as Jesus sees and know what He knows. When you look at others, you don't see their actions and equate those behaviors with their identity. Instead, you see them through His eyes and respond based on who He created them to be. You fight for the reclamation of their identity in the heavenlies, wrestling with the enemy to wrench them out of his clutches, your love for them empowering your prayers on their behalf.

Fear, which is just another word for doubt, dissipates like the smoky illusion it has always been, for "fear has to do with punishment" (I John 4:18), and you *know* (faith is certain knowledge of what is unseen – Hebrews 11:1) the evidence against you has been excluded, and your case has been thrown out. Along with your fear/doubt, the cloak of shame lifts off you because you have been defended by Jesus Christ, found not guilty by the Righteous Judge, and walked out of the courtroom in complete freedom.

Your view of the worldly realm also changes. No longer desiring the things valued by the world (attention, power, status, control, safety, security, money, prestige, acclaim, position, comfort, ease of life), you seek first the Kingdom and His righteousness (Matthew 6:33) and trust Him for what else you may need. Love becomes your primary motivation as your heart grows to match His.

You transition from living in the temporal plain to the spiritual plane, or from being of the world into living in the Kingdom. Remember, Jesus said the Kingdom is here and now, within you, not just some future place to get to later. The Kingdom is available to you in the present. The question is, where do you choose to live? Do you focus your attention and valuing on the worldly plain? Or do you fix your eyes on Jesus and live in His "unseen" realm? (II Corinthians 4:18, Hebrews 12:2). Spiritual maturation means seeing yourself, others, and the world through the eyes of Christ, with spiritual lenses, allowing you to see beyond how things appear in the temporal view, seeing instead in truth, as He sees.

PERFECTION

Jesus ends a discourse on love, specifically loving those you don't want to love (your enemies, those who persecute you, those who don't love you) with the admonition, "Be perfect, therefore, as your heavenly Father is perfect" (Matthew 5:48). Most read this verse and immediately start scrambling for what they must "do" to "be" perfect, but in so doing, they miss the point Jesus is making here.

If you could "do" perfect, you could follow the law perfectly, and Christ would never have had to come. But as discussed, the law exposed our sin, our inability, and our need for Christ, and it was necessary for Christ to come. Clearly, you cannot "do" perfect, and Jesus isn't asking you to. So, what does He mean?

If you step outside the physical, worldly realm into the spiritual plane, what do you see? Your flesh, still bound to this world and tied to sin, is left behind. Your sins, covered by the blood of Christ, are gone, remembered no more (Isaiah 43:25, Jeremiah 31:34, Hebrews 8:12, 10:17). What's left?

Your God-created nature, the spirit He knit together as your unique identity, is what remains. Untainted by sin, untouched by the world, your true nature is perfectly who He wanted you to be. Yes, you are not God, so you don't have everything of God contained within you. You reflect aspects of His nature, and pieces are missing where you are lacking certain other aspects – thus, your need for God to abide within you and become one with you, to complete you. However, you are exactly who He created, perfectly as He made you to be; you might say, perfectly imperfect.

The treasure of your perfectly imperfect self is still contained in a "jar of clay" (II Corinthians 4:7), as Paul describes it, and the clay jar remains cracked and flawed and fragile because it remains bound to this fallen world. The container that is your body is destined to perish, for "what you sow does not come to life unless it dies. The body that is sown is perishable, it is raised imperishable; it is sown in dishonor, it is raised in glory; it is sown in weakness, it is raised in power; it is sown a natural body, it is raised a spiritual body" (I Corinthians 15:36, 42-44). As Jesus said, "the Spirit gives life; the flesh counts for nothing" (John 6:63). You are sanctified in your spirit, but your body, made of the substance of this sin-infused world, must die so you can be raised, as Jesus was raised, with a new kind of body.

Yet, while you remain bound in this worldly body, "the flesh desires what is contrary to the Spirit, and the Spirit what is contrary to the flesh. They are in conflict with each other, so that you are not to do whatever you want" (Galatians 5:17). You are instructed to "live according to the Spirit" (Romans 8:5) instead of listening to and following the desires of the flesh. Living according to the Spirit brings life and peace (Romans 8:6). Through connection with His presence and conversation with Him, you align yourself with His Spirit, believing and trusting what He tells you and shows you, so you are better able to walk out His path in faith.

You will stumble. You will fall. Paul describes it this way: "I do not understand what I do. For what I want to do I do not do, but what I hate I do" (Romans 7:15). But the failings of the flesh do not undermine your sanctification, as Paul goes on to say, "Who will rescue me from this body that is subject to death? Thanks be to God, who delivers me through Jesus Christ our Lord!" (Romans 7:24-25).

Your spirit, united with His, remains pure and holy, even while your body perishes due to sin. Therefore, sin no longer carries any weight beyond the flesh and the consequences the sin produces in this world. Don't give it weight by believing it reflects something about your true self. As Paul explained, "it is no longer I myself who do it, but it is sin living in me (meaning in the flesh)" (Romans 7:17). His cleansing blood has sanctified your spirit once and for all.

PASSING JUDGMENT

You have been made holy and sanctified, not by any work on your part but by the "all-surpassing power" of Jesus Christ (II Corinthians 4:7); therefore, you have no position from which to pass judgment on yourself or others. Jesus was clear when He said, "Do not judge, and you will not be judged. Do not condemn, and you will not be condemned. Forgive, and you will be forgiven" (Luke 6:37). These verses apply to how you see yourself and how you see others, for if you judge, you are presuming you have greater knowledge and wisdom and insight and understanding than God.

If, in your free will, you assume the role of judge, you choose to replace God's judgment with your own, and as discussed, God respects the choices you make in your freedom to choose. So, if you judge, He allows your judgment to stand against you. If you choose to condemn, even though there is no condemnation for those in Christ (Romans 8:1), your condemnation will stand. By your own hand you are judged and condemned, not by God.

Similarly, if you forgive, your forgiveness stands, but if you do not, by your choice to withhold forgiveness you lose forgiveness. Look at the parable of the unmerciful servant (Matthew 18:23-35). A servant (let's call him Bob), jailed because of his debt, has his debt forgiven by the gracious master. As soon as Bob is released, he seeks out a fellow servant (we'll call him Dan) who owes Bob some money and demands payment. When Dan can't repay, Bob has poor Dan thrown in prison. The master, hearing of this injustice, issues the same judgment to Bob that Bob gave to Dan. In this case, Bob determined his own consequences based on his judgment against Dan.

So, what was Bob's prison? He was bound by his judgment and lack of forgiveness to the debt he owed (in other words, his own sin), which he could never pay off, and which had already been forgiven. Because Bob chose to hold judgment against Dan, he reaped judgment on himself for his own debts. The forgiveness was negated because of his own unforgiveness of the exact same debt in another. Although Bob's sin was expunged, he bound himself to

Dan's debt (sin) through his judgment, leaving himself once again imprisoned.

Having received the greatness of the mercy of the master for all of his substantial debt, did Bob truly understand the depth of the master's forgiveness if he was holding Dan accountable to pay for his debts? As you examine your heart for judgment and unforgiveness, ask yourself the same question. Do you truly understand how much you have been forgiven and how wondrous your freedom from the courtroom really is, if you continue to judge yourself, or you judge someone else for their sins and find them guilty? Do you truly understand what Christ's blood has bought, or are you negating the value of what He has done for you?

DEPENDENCE ON FAITH

The beautiful jewels discussed in this chapter – confidence before His throne, freedom from fear and shame, love made complete in you, an answer for the accuser, evidentiary exclusion and a not-guilty verdict, the fulfillment of the requirements of the law, spiritual maturity, and perfection – are all gifts from Jesus, elements of the treasure of sanctification. Jesus offers these gifts freely, but your reception of these gifts rests on one thing: faith.

If you choose to see through worldly eyes, you may not see any evidence of these gifts The enemy continues to accuse you, and external circumstances continuously point to reasons for you to fear and feel shame, your failures and imperfections, and the need for you to 'do more' and 'get it right' to be 'good enough.' However, "we live by faith, not by sight" (II Corinthians 5:7).

Also, if you look to Jesus to 'fix' your circumstances, and use those results to prove His faithfulness, your faith will be shaken, and you will find yourself scrambling to justify outcomes you didn't want with tortured explanations like "God is a mystery" or "He must have a higher purpose that matters more than I do." Many are shipwrecked by painful outcomes and become angry at God, even rejecting Him, because they look to the circumstances as proof of God answering prayers or look to Him to 'fix' the circumstances instead of to redeem them. Remember, Jesus never promised to 'fix' things circumstantially. What He promised, and what He demonstrates, is He walks through those circumstances with you, strengthens you in them to remain in His peace, and shields and protects your spirit with His presence and truth. "So we fix our eyes not on what is seen, but on what is unseen, since what is seen is temporary, but what is unseen is eternal" (II Corinthians 4:18).

Faith is not wishful thinking. It isn't crossing your fingers and trying to convince yourself to believe. Faith is certain knowledge of the unseen based on personal experiences of the unseen. For example, you can't see gravity; however, you experience the results of the presence of gravity every day, and when you get out of bed, you don't question whether gravity is going to successfully hold you to the earth, just because you can't see it. Instead, you believe it is real, you trust it to hold you, and you get out of bed (act), confident you will not float away. In fact, when you consider it, you realize the question of gravity's reality never crosses your mind. You simply walk out expecting without question or doubt to remain connected to the earth. That is Hebrews 11:1 faith.

The writer of Hebrews goes on to offer a 40-verse discourse on the results of faith throughout Scripture. Each story highlights the things that came through their faith; yet, as the writer explains,

151

"They did not receive the things promised; they only saw them and welcomed them from a distance" (Hebrews 11:13). These many individuals lived by faith and not by sight. They believed and trusted God, and acted on that trust, and their faith was credited to them as righteousness (Romans 4:3, 5 22-25). Yes, "these were all commended for their faith, yet none of them received what had been promised" (Hebrews 11:39).

You, on the other hand, have received what was promised, the Kingdom of God, and everything that comes with His Kingdom. His presence, His love, His truth – these things are of significance. They are eternal. But worldly outcomes and external circumstances are transient and temporary. "The world and its desires pass away" (I John 2:17) – "the old order of things" will pass away (Revelation 21:4) – "heaven and earth will pass away" (Mark 13:31), but His love, His truth, and His presence remain.

Without faith, you will believe what your eyes see (physical realm) instead of the unseen (spiritual realm). But by faith, you can have the eyes to see as He sees, because faith gives you the knowledge of things unseen. You don't have to be focused on or phased by the circumstances surrounding you. You don't have to be fearful of what you do or do not see. You don't have to hide yourself behind walls, protect yourself from potential hurts, or run away from difficulties. Knowing (by faith) who you are in Christ and knowing (by faith) He is present with you, strengthening you for whatever may come, becomes your shield wall and hiding place.

Jesus told a parable about faith. Notice He begins the parable talking about those who hear His words, then believe and trust Him enough to put them into practice (act) – in other words, He is describing faith. "Therefore, everyone who hears these words

152

of mine and puts them into practice is like a wise man who built his house on the rock. The rain came down, the streams rose, and the winds blew and beat against that house; yet it did not fall, because it had its foundation on the rock. But everyone who hears these words of mine and does not put them into practice is like a foolish man who built his house on sand. The rain came down, the streams rose, and the winds blew and beat against that house, and it fell with a great crash." (Matthew 7:24-27).

Do you build on what is certain and eternal, or what is temporal and physical? If you build your life on the rock of Jesus Christ, your house can stand any flood or storm. Your circumstances do not alarm you because you know your foundation is solid and can withstand anything. But, as Jesus said, if you rely on those things that are shifting sand beneath your feet, the ever-changing and uncertain physical, worldly realm, as your security, as soon as circumstances grow threatening, your house will fall.

Doubt, then, is a serious matter. As mentioned before, fear is just another word for doubt, so fear is also a serious threat to your spiritual house. You may consider fear benign and doubt inevitable, but they are actually deadly. Doubt prevents you from receiving the gifts of the treasure of sanctification. Doubt clouds your ability to see Jesus and your own identity, returns the cloak of shame over your head, and sends you running back into the courtroom to face charges again, as if you have not already been set free. Faith secures your house, opens your eyes, and allows you to experience the freedom the Righteous Judge has already provided by excluding the evidence against you and throwing your case out of court.

CONCLUSION

153

Because of the blood of Jesus, you are free to embrace the verdict of the Righteous Judge, step down from the judgment seat and out of the role of defendant, and reject the accusations of the enemy against you. Jesus can lift the cloak of shame, and you can walk out of your prison and into the light of true freedom. With full understanding of the extent of the mercy given to you by Jesus, you are able to offer that same mercy through Christ to yourself and others. Because you are sanctified, made holy and pure by the blood of Jesus, you are able to walk the path of spiritual maturity, guided by the principles of righteousness, justice, and love instead of remaining bound to the law. You begin to see as Jesus sees and know as He knows, living in the spiritual realm more and focusing on the worldly realm less.

You are made perfect in your spirit, even in the midst of the failings of your flesh, so you can, with belief and trust, stand before the throne of God with confidence. Because you are sanctified, you are:

Free to stand face to face, eye to eye, with Jesus without judgment or the covering of the cloak of shame;

Free to reject the enemy's accusations and lies, relying only on the truth of Christ;

Free to approach God's throne boldly, assured of the perfection of your created being, your spirit;

Free to see others through Christ's eyes and offer them the grace offered freely to you;

Free to grow into maturity and seek wisdom, righteousness, justice, love, and the deeper things of faith;

Free from being bound to the flesh and its worldly desires, and putting aside those desires, to live in the Kingdom;

Free to stand on the certain knowledge of faith, not looking to your circumstances but looking only to Jesus.

Peace comes from standing on the solid Rock of Jesus Christ, no matter your circumstances, believing His words, trusting His goodness, and acting on what you know is true. Joy comes from fear dissipating and the cloak of shame lifting because of His love and His ongoing presence. Your sanctification and the gifts that accompany it are like the shining jewels described as making up the gates of His Kingdom.

STARTING POINT: QUESTIONS TO EXPLORE SANCTIFICATION

Answer the following questions to further explore the sanctification Jesus has secured. Consider your answers prayerfully and thoughtfully. Don't offer a superficial response and move on to the next question but look deeply within and be as honest with yourself as you can be. Avoid giving "pat" answers you might have heard in church, particularly if you've not examined what those responses mean in depth. These questions are designed to help you understand your state of being in His Kingdom and experience true freedom from judgment.

1. What have you imagined God would say to you when you came before His throne for judgment? What do you believe He will say now?
2. How has your cloak of shame impacted your view of yourself, of others, and of God?

3. In what ways are you like Christ? (Look to how He described your identity and see how you reflect His nature).
4. What has Satan accused you of before the judge (you), and what evidence has he used against you?
5. In what ways have you bound yourself again to the law?
6. What worldly things try to garner your attention or desire?
7. What judgments have you held against others? How are those judgments similar to judgments you've made against yourself?
8. What are the doubts and fears that rise up in you? When do they typically trouble you?
9. What are times you have looked beyond your circumstances and outcomes and trusted God with whatever was to come?
10. What "jewels" of sanctification are you able to see within yourself?

Destination: Prayers for Spiritual Maturity

Find a quiet place with few distractions to sit with Jesus. Still your mind and quiet your heart by repeating a verse of Scripture meaningful to you; for example, you could repeat, "I am saved through the sanctifying work of the Spirit and through belief in the truth" (II Thessalonians 2:13). I have written a prayer for you as an example, but use your own words, from your heart, to ask Jesus to reveal His sanctification: *Lord, you have told me I am sanctified by your blood, the presence of your Spirit, and your truth, but sometimes the enemy tries to say I am guilty. He is constantly accusing me of doing wrong things and not being good enough for you. He keeps trotting out all this evidence against me, and I don't know how to respond. Would you please respond to the enemy's accusations? And would you help believe and trust in your sanctifying work in my spirit?*

After you pray, spend time in silent meditation, eyes closed and listening for His answers. He may show you an image in your mind, or you may hear words or phrases in your mind, or you may sense emotions or experiences He brings to you to reveal His sanctification. He might bring to mind a particular verse or story from Scripture that reveals some truth you need to counter the enemy's accusations. You can recognize responses from the Lord by the peace they stir up in your heart. If an image or word comes to you that brings anxiety or shame, reject it, recenter yourself on Jesus, and ask again. If you think you hear a response that contradicts Scripture, pray against enemy interference, recenter on Jesus, and ask again. Otherwise, don't analyze what comes up or question if it's the Lord. Instead, go with it and follow wherever He takes you. If you are getting "off base," He will let you know. Keep with it, asking Jesus to explain anything you don't understand and to show you more, until you feel He is finished.

If you don't hear anything, don't be concerned or frustrated. Remember, we have an enemy who actively opposes our treasure seeking and tries to thwart our relationship with Jesus. Take a break and come back to your prayer later. This time, if you don't receive a response, ask Jesus what is in the way. It may be a lie you believe, such as you are unworthy to come face to face with Jesus, or you may be agreeing with the accusations of the enemy and your own agreement is getting in your way. False beliefs about God can also hinder making a connection; for example, seeing God as harsh, punishing, and full of wrath against you. Whatever Jesus reveals is in the way, ask Him to bring truth to your heart to move the hindrance out of your way. Then return to your prayer request.

Another prayer you could pursue is asking Jesus to deepen your spiritual maturity. An example of this type of prayer would be: *Lord, I am solid on the elementary aspects of my faith. I know about your death in my stead and how your resurrection defeated death, so I can have eternal life. Now, I want to know more. I want to understand the deeper things of faith. I want to experience more and more in my relationship with you. I want to receive wisdom and truth in all things. I desire to pursue your righteousness. Would you help me to understand and receive the deeper truths and experience the depths of your love for me to the fullest?* This type of prayer will be an ongoing process, as spiritual maturity is never finished and continues through to the point of your going home, so keep seeking the answers from Jesus to these requests. Open your heart to greater and more experiences with Him.

Finally, you could pray for Jesus to help you expel all doubt and deepen your faith. Your prayer could be: *Lord, I believe what you say is true. I trust you as much as I am able, and I am willing to learn to trust you more. I understand faith is joining action to my belief and trust, but I struggle with putting my belief and trust into action. Would you help me to come to the place where my faith in you looks the same as my faith in gravity? Please help my certainty in everything you promise and my knowledge of the unseen realm. What do I need to understand to be fully vested in my faith?* Listen for His responses to your requests. Don't be surprised if He responds in unexpected ways – He is, after all, working on building your faith.

158

As always, remember Jesus is your partner in this endeavor of spiritual maturity. He has sanctified you by His blood, so that work is finished. He has declared the evidence against you as inadmissible and has rendered the verdict as not guilty, setting you free from the charges against you. That work is also complete. Now, the building of your faith and the deepening of your maturity becomes your shared process and focus. Your humility in accepting you cannot achieve sanctification, perfect your faith, or reach spiritual maturity on your own will help you to be more open to receive His gifts.

SETTING THE COURSE: LIVING IN HIS SANCTIFICATION

The first section presents concepts you may want to internalize, and the second section lists some actions you may take to apply the information you have studied. Approach the following concepts and actions prayerfully. Avoid any thinking that you must rigidly adhere to them, because these are only suggestions and may not work for you. Everyone is different. Remember, your sanctification has been accomplished by Jesus' work on the cross, and your maturity isn't up to you alone but is established in partnership with Christ. Use these suggestions to deepen your relationship with Him in your quest to live the Kingdom life.

INTERNALIZE THE CONCEPTS

Consider the implications of the enemy's accusations being disallowed and the evidence presented against you excluded. Contemplate what it means to walk free from the courtroom with all charges against you dropped.

159

Meditate on what it means to be able to step down from the judgment seat. Examine the impact of allowing God to be the Righteous Judge on how you see yourself and others.

Consider the impact the cloak of shame has had on your life and your relationship with God. Visualize the cloak lifting from you as the light of God bathes you in His love.

Contemplate your freedom from bondage to the law. Evaluate your motives in choosing your actions in the absence of the law's direction. Consider how God's presence will impact your choices.

Meditate on the war between your spirit and your flesh. Consider how this war is in evidence in your life. Examine ways to respond appropriately to the flesh.

Contemplate the treasure of sanctification and the jewels given to you by God through that gift. Contrast the worldly offerings with the offerings of the Spirit.

Evaluate your faith, defined as the certain knowledge of the unseen. Meditate on those truths you believe, trust, and act upon in your life. Examine ways doubt has impacted your relationship with God.

PROCESS THEIR APPLICATION

Develop a close-knit community of others seeking spiritual growth and maturity. Through prayer together and sharing what you are learning and hearing from Jesus, support each other and affirm each other in your growth process. Maintain your connections through consistent contact, making it a point to share new revelations as they come from the Lord.

Pray specifically against shame and fear. Ask Jesus to reveal to you the specific beliefs behind your shame and fear and the sources of those beliefs. Then, ask Jesus for truth to replace those beliefs. Open your heart and mind, remaining quiet and still until you receive something from Jesus. This may take many different forms, because it will be very personal, but your heart will recognize His 'voice' and will respond by feeling lighter, freer, and more at peace.

Make a list of areas where doubt has been a problem for you. List these doubts in one column. Ask Jesus to help you identify the reasons for your doubts, paying special attention to places where you have used circumstances to judge God's faithfulness and goodness. Then, attack each doubt, one at a time; first by asking forgiveness for the doubt; next, by asking for Jesus to help you with that doubt; and finally, by listing experiences with God that directly challenge that doubt in a second parallel column. When you complete the process with one doubt, move on to the next one on your list. As each doubt begins to fade and disappear, erase the doubt from your list until all that is left is your list of experiences with God.

Read Scriptures specifically related to the deeper things of faith, including wisdom Scriptures (Proverbs, for example), righteousness Scriptures (Romans, for example), and love

Scriptures (John, for example). Prayerfully consider the lessons of the verses as you read them, asking Jesus to write these truths on your heart. Discuss these verses with Him and seek with Him deeper understanding and applications for these verses.

When you find yourself getting caught up in your flesh (the worldly self), identify what is happening. You can tell when it happens because you will begin to feel anxiety, shame, self-pity, and/or unrighteous, self-centered anger and frustration. This response can show up in the smallest, least significant areas (in response to others' driving, for example) to very important areas (being tempted to sin against those you love, for example). Once you've identified what is happening, remove yourself from where you are to a private space. Pray for help. Take five steps back (in your mind) from the situation you are in and ask Jesus to reveal where you got tripped up or snared by the enemy. Then, return to a spiritual truth you are certain is true, something that is rock solid and sure in your heart. (You might use your truth journal to help you with this part of the process). This can be a truth you've learned directly from the Holy Spirit or something you've read in Scripture that made a significant impact on you. Finally, process the worldly circumstance that snared you in light of the spiritual truth(s) revealed by Jesus.

SIX

The Treasure of Wisdom

YOUR COMPASS

Consider it pure joy, my brothers and sisters, whenever you face trials of many kinds, because you know that the testing of your faith produces perseverance. Let perseverance finish its work so that you may be mature and complete, not lacking anything. If any of you lacks wisdom, you should ask God, who gives generously to all without finding fault, and it will be given to you (James 1:2-5).

Show your wisdom and understanding to the nations, who will hear about all these decrees and say, "Surely this great nation is a wise and understanding people." What other nation is so great as to have their gods near them the way the LORD our God is near us whenever we pray to him? (Deuteronomy 4:6-7).

But where can wisdom be found? Where does understanding dwell? No mortal comprehends its worth; it cannot be found in the land of the living. It cannot be bought with the finest gold, nor can its price be weighed out in silver. Where then does wisdom come from?

Where does understanding dwell? It is hidden from the eyes of every living thing, concealed even from the birds in the sky. God understands the way to it and he alone knows where it dwells...he said to the human race, "The fear of the Lord—that is wisdom, and to shun evil is understanding." (Job 28:12-13, 15, 20-21, 23, 28).

If you accept my words and store up my commands within you, turning your ear to wisdom and applying your heart to understanding—indeed, if you call out for insight and cry aloud for understanding, and if you look for it as for silver and search for it as for hidden treasure, then you will understand the fear of the LORD and find the knowledge of God. For the LORD gives wisdom; from his mouth come knowledge and understanding. (Proverbs 2:1-6).

For the message of the cross is foolishness to those who are perishing, but to us who are being saved it is the power of God. For it is written: "I will destroy the wisdom of the wise; the intelligence of the intelligent I will frustrate." Where is the wise person? Where is the teacher of the law? Where is the philosopher of this age? Has not God made foolish the wisdom of the world? For since in the wisdom of God the world through its wisdom did not know him, God was pleased through the foolishness of what was preached to save those who believe. Jews demand signs and Greeks look for wisdom, but we preach Christ crucified: a stumbling block to Jews and foolishness to Gentiles, but to those whom God has called, both Jews and Greeks, Christ the power of God and the wisdom of God. For the foolishness of God is wiser than human wisdom, and the weakness of God is stronger than human strength. (I Corinthians 1:18-25).

I keep asking that the God of our Lord Jesus Christ, the glorious Father, may give you the Spirit of wisdom and revelation, so that you may know him better (Ephesians 1:17).

Who is wise and understanding among you? Let them show it by their good life, by deeds done in the humility that comes from wisdom. But if you harbor bitter envy and selfish ambition in your hearts, do not boast about it or deny the truth. Such "wisdom" does not come down from heaven but is earthly, unspiritual, demonic. For where you have envy and selfish ambition, there you find disorder and every evil practice. But the wisdom that comes from heaven is first of all pure; then peace-loving, considerate, submissive, full of mercy and good fruit, impartial and sincere (James 3:13-17).

For with much wisdom comes much sorrow; the more knowledge, the more grief (Ecclesiastes 1:18).

MAP KEY: DISCERNING COSTUME JEWELRY

WISDOM DEFINED

True wisdom is light from God.

But the enemy, the great counterfeiter, likes to flash shiny, sparkling costume jewelry, claiming his paste is valuable wisdom and knowledge and distracting you from the true treasure of wisdom given by God.

Wisdom is best defined as the ability to discern inner traits, having insight, and having the qualities of experience, knowledge, and good judgment. Notice from this definition that wisdom is about sight, both outward vision into others and inward vision into yourself. Wisdom is seeing beyond the superficial, looking beneath the surface to the process level of understanding; in other words, seeing into the heart (yours and others) to discern motives, values, beliefs, and the deeper movements and meanings of life.

If wisdom is about sight, then a lack of wisdom is a form of blindness. Although you aren't aware of it, you were born blind. Without Jesus, you would remain blind throughout your life. You wander through life in darkness, stumbling and slamming into walls – then you act surprised that the wall was there, because you think you see where you're going. Given that perspective, you then blame others for your faltering steps, or blame the wall for being there, or blame circumstances for putting you in a situation where the obstacles were in your way. Rarely do you realize your own blindness caused your fall.

But the truth is, as this Scripture in Isaiah 42:6-7 & 16 indicates, you are indeed blind: "I, the LORD, have called you in righteousness; I will take hold of your hand…to open eyes that are blind, to free captives from prison, and to release from the dungeon those who sit in darkness. I will lead the blind by ways they have not known, along unfamiliar paths I will guide them; I will turn the darkness into light before them and make the rough places smooth. These are the things I will do; I will not forsake them." Without the light of God, you will stumble; you will fall; you will crash into wall after wall.

And don't think, if you are a believer in Jesus, you cannot be blinded. Christians, too, can be easily blinded. No one is immune to the effects of the darkness. When you walk on the path of your own choosing (self-sufficiency), walking on unfamiliar paths without your Guide (self-determination), or getting distracted from focusing on Jesus every step of the way (self-centeredness), don't be surprised when things go awry. Darkness waits closely for you around every corner. The enemy, the prowling lion (I Peter 5:8), is lurking in the darkness – his arena – licking his chops as you stumble along your own road and away from God's guiding presence and voice. He quickly devours you, destroying everything he can in as short a period of time as possible, and it doesn't take long for you to crash and burn. Can you see why Jesus gave so many examples in His healings of giving sight to the blind, so you could understand His role in your life?

Jesus described Himself as the "light of the world" (John 8:12). Without Him, this world has no light. "For God, who said, 'Let light shine out of darkness,' made his light shine in our hearts to give us the light of the knowledge of God's glory displayed in the face of Christ" (II Corinthians 4:6). The Isaiah 42 verses referenced above, and many other Scriptures tell you that God's will for you is to be in the light with Him, walking side by side with Him as your partner and your first love, listening to His guiding voice and following His well-lit path.

But you always have a choice. You can listen to His voice and hold tight to His hand, or you can set out on your own. You can fix your eyes on Jesus and stay close by His side, or you can choose to act as your own god. If you choose to walk on your own, don't be surprised when you crash into a wall or fall over obstacles that you did not expect and did not see. Before you take off on your own, keep in mind, you are blind without His light.

Paul draws a sharp contrast between the so-called wisdom of the world and God's wisdom, saying, "God made foolish the wisdom of the world" (I Corinthians 1:20), and, "Do not deceive yourselves. If any of you think you are wise by the standards of this age, you should become 'fools' so that you may become wise. For the wisdom of this world is foolishness in God's sight" (I Corinthians 3:18-19). For Paul, the only true wisdom is belonging wholly and completely to Christ (I Corinthians 3:23).

What does Paul mean by the wisdom of the world? As an educated man, he would've been exposed to Greek philosophies, such as those which gave rise to such English words as logic, stoic, cynic, epicurean, and eclectic, and developed the Socratic method of teaching and the scientific method of research. He would also be familiar with the Jewish methods of debating Scripture and philosophy. Paul himself used those debate techniques to argue for the gospel. Yet, he called such things foolishness in God's sight.

The wisdom of the world looks to the creation to understand created things, but trying to understand purpose, meaning, processes, death, truth, and other such "big picture" questions of life by looking to the physical world for explanation can only go so far. You can extrapolate some things by starting with the present physical reality and deducing certain origins, but this process is inherently limited. In addition, the absence of the inclusion of the spiritual realm (the unseen) is a major limitation to the wisdom of the world.

Doesn't it make more sense to look to the Creator rather than looking to His creation for wisdom? The created thing, including humankind, cannot access or comprehend the mind and heart of its Creator, His reasons or purposes or motives or thought processes, unless His mind and heart are revealed by the Creator Himself. Enlightenment can only come from the Source of all light.

Isaiah 42 goes on to reveal the reasons for the blind and deaf state of humankind: "Hear, you deaf; look, you blind, and see! You have seen many things, but you pay no attention; your ears are open, but you do not listen…this is a people plundered and looted, all of them trapped in pits or hidden away in prisons. They have become plunder" (Isaiah 42:18, 20, 22). The so-called wisdom of the world leaves you trapped in pits and hidden away in prisons. The wisdom of the world would tell you to protect yourself, because pain is bad, and suffering should be avoided at all costs. The wisdom of the world would tell you to take the easier of the paths available to you, because easy is better than hard. The wisdom of the world would say put yourself first, think of yourself before others, meet your needs first, and seek safety and security above all else. The wisdom of the world would say fear will protect you and worry will prepare you before bad things happen, so you won't be blindsided. The wisdom of the world would instruct you to build strong walls around yourself, and to hide your true self and put on a mask that others find pleasing, so you won't be rejected. The wisdom of the world would reject hope in fear of being disappointed. Do you see the pits and prisons?

The world's wisdom opposes and hinders everything leading to Godly wisdom. For example, if you choose self-protection over love, you lose the richness of relationships and the opportunities for growth that come, even through the pain of loss. If you choose the easy road rather than the narrow way, you miss the learning experiences you gain from the struggle and the insights those moments bring you. If you make yourself the center of your universe, you limit your growth to your own perception. If safety and security are your idols and fear is your guide, you will find yourself trapped into creating what you most fear, a self-fulfilling prophesy.

God's wisdom doesn't venerate easy or safe or self-focus. God's wisdom doesn't fear pain or hardship; it doesn't look to the circumstances to determine what is good and right and true, or to determine how to feel. God's wisdom embraces hope and openness and honors the true self, the created self. God's wisdom is found in centering your life on Him alone, walking with Him as your genuine self through everything, no matter how difficult or painful. Your experiences with Him help you gain insight, and He provides enlightenment and truth through His presence in the midst of it all.

Where are you trapped? How are you hidden away in a prison of your own making?

WISDOM SOURCES

Three foundational truths undergird your understanding of wisdom: 1) all true wisdom originates with God; 2) the more wisdom you receive from God, the more you understand how little you know and how "foolish" (to use Paul's term for the wisdom of the world) you were and are; and, 3) wisdom is key to spiritual maturity.

God is the source of all wisdom ("Oh, the depth of the riches of the wisdom and knowledge of God!" – Romans 11:33), and He uses different vehicles to deliver His wisdom to you. Some of those means may surprise you.

His first delivery system is your mistakes. Only God, your Redeemer, could find a way to turn your mistakes into something as great as the development of wisdom. Consider the Proverbs, which contrast folly and wisdom, point out the mistakes you might make and their consequences, and describe the responses indicative of wisdom. These verses repeatedly demonstrate the built-in learning system created by God – choices and consequences. As Paul explains, "Do not be deceived: God cannot be mocked. A man reaps what he sows" (Galatians 6:7). God has designed creation itself to teach you wisdom from your mistakes through the process of reaping and sowing, choice and consequence.

Here are several examples from Proverbs presenting how choices produce consequences: "If you are wise, your wisdom will reward you" (Proverbs 9:12); "The wages of the righteous is life, but the earnings of the wicked are sin and death" (Proverbs 10:16); "Trouble pursues the sinner, but the righteous are rewarded with good things" (Proverbs 13:21); "When justice is done, it brings joy to the righteous but terror to evildoers" (Proverbs 21:15); "The faithless will be fully repaid for their ways, and the good rewarded for theirs" (Proverbs 14:14); "What the wicked dread will overtake them; what the righteous desire will be granted" (Proverbs 10:24); "The evil deeds of the wicked ensnare them; the cords of their sins hold them fast. For lack of discipline they will die, led astray by their own great folly" (Proverbs 5:22-23); "Whoever pursues righteousness and love finds life, prosperity and honor" (Proverbs 21:21). God's system of reaping and sowing provides continual opportunities for learning and developing wisdom.

Of course, it is possible to miss the lessons of your mistakes. You could try to circumvent the consequences or avoid them, you could refuse or ignore their lessons, or you could blame others or blame God instead of taking responsibility for your choice and its consequences, as Proverbs 19:3 describes: "A person's own folly leads to their ruin, yet their heart rages against the LORD." But if you approach your mistakes without shame and recognize them as a chance to gain wisdom, consequences become a wonderful tool for growth and learning, and mistakes become opportunities. So, you can see here how shame is a tool of the enemy that keeps you from growing in wisdom.

Another vehicle for delivering wisdom from the Lord is adversity. Now, please do not misunderstand me. I am not suggesting the Lord inflicts hardship on you to "teach you a lesson" – far from it. The enemy is the one who delights in bringing hardship, along with the difficulties that come from our own poor choices, the poor choices of others, and the tainting presence of sin in this world. However, God is your Redeemer. He takes what Satan intends for evil and turns it for good. Through adversity, you learn perseverance, develop character, and build hope (Romans 5:3-4), all of which grow you in wisdom. As James 1:4 states, "Let perseverance finish its work so that you may be mature and complete, not lacking anything."

Wisdom also comes through knowing God. Notice I didn't say knowledge about God. Knowing God comes through time spent in connection and communication with Him, just like you come to know a new friend or build an intimate relationship. You don't talk "at" your friend to get to know them; instead, you listen to them, and you share experiences with them. You allow them to tell you

172

about themselves, and you share yourself in turn. You don't grow a relationship by making demands. What kind of relationship would you develop if all you did was take from the other? Relationships are mutual; they don't exist when one person does all the giving and the other does all the taking. You also don't expect to form a deep relationship through an occasional meeting or superficial conversation. Intimate partners want to spend as much time together as possible. They share from their hearts, expose their deepest feelings, from the most painful to the most joyous, and keep no secrets from each other. They don't feel the need to put up walls or pretend to be something they are not.

The same is true of your relationship with Jesus. Sharing your deepest heart, opening up the places in yourself no one else is allowed to see, welcoming Him into your pain and your joy, and spending all your time in communion with Him fosters knowing Him truly, deeply, intimately. Through knowing Him in this way, you come to know God, for, as Jesus said, "If you really know me, you will know my Father as well" (John 14:7). As you absorb more of what Jesus knows, you are exposed to God's wisdom, and through those experiences you gain wisdom.

Reverence for the Lord is the natural outflow of knowing God and another source of wisdom. "The fear of the Lord is the beginning of wisdom, and knowledge of the Holy One is understanding" (Proverbs 9:10). When "fear of the Lord" is referenced in Scripture, it doesn't refer to being afraid of God; the intended meaning is reverence for God, recognizing God's holiness, and responding with appropriate humility and awe in His presence. As Proverbs 22:4 states, "Humility is the fear of the Lord; its wages are riches and honor and life." Similarly, Hebrews 12:28 says,

173

"Therefore, since we are receiving a kingdom that cannot be shaken, let us be thankful, and so worship God acceptably with reverence and awe." Because of the immeasurable and all-encompassing wonder of the treasures of His Kingdom, given freely to you, true awareness of these many treasures results in reverence, and reverence produces wisdom.

Spiritual warfare, the ongoing battle against the enemy, is another source of wisdom. The more you practice discerning good from evil, and the more clarity you gain in identifying what is good and right and true from what is destruction, falsehood, and lies, the more wisdom you develop. However, without the presence of His Spirit within you and His truth revealed to your heart, you will be blind to the machinations of evil. Evil will look like good to you, and good evil (Isaiah 5:20). The cunning and sinister whispers of the enemy will seem like truth.

The enemy doesn't typically come at you with a frontal assault against your core values, although he certainly could and might. But his preferred method of attack is to take a truth, particularly one that 'sounds' Biblical, twist it just a little so it's one degree off, convince you it's truth, and encourage you to pursue walking in it as if it is truth. The farther you walk forward, the father away from truth you go. "So justice is far from us, and righteousness does not reach us. We look for light, but all is darkness; for brightness, but we walk in deep shadows… uttering lies our hearts have conceived. So justice is driven back, and righteousness stands at a distance; truth has stumbled in the streets, honesty cannot enter. Truth is nowhere to be found, and whoever shuns evil becomes a prey" (Isaiah 59:9, 13-15).

Another enemy strategy is to interpret your perceptions of your circumstances and experiences for you with lies, thus making the lies 'feel' true. A simple illustration of this tactic is how the enemy might tell a second born child, who, in reality, can never quite catch up to the older sibling, that their failure to match their sibling's skill or ability is proof they are not and will never be good enough. The false seed is planted. Then, the enemy follows up with reinterpretation of future stumbles as additional proof text, and the lie, "I'm not good enough," is sealed deep in the individual's heart.

These embedded lies block wisdom. Wisdom opposes false beliefs, but the enemy has sown seeds that feel true. Thus, "When anyone hears the message about the kingdom and does not understand it, the evil one comes and snatches away what was sown in their heart" (Matthew 13:19).

According to Hebrews 5:14, the mature, "by constant use have trained themselves to distinguish good from evil." Discernment is like any muscle – it develops with use and practice. So, how do you discern the difference between truth and lie? First and foremost, you will know it by its fruit (Matthew 12:33, Luke 6:44). In other words, what grows out of it? What does the seed produce on the tree? Does the fruit of the Spirit grow from the seeds planted? (Galatians 5:22-23). If so, the seed is good. If not, the seed is not from God and needs to be rejected. Does a thought produce anxiety or fear or shame? If so, that thought is a lie from the evil one. Does a belief produce self-loathing, hatred of self or others, or judgment of self or others? If so, reject the belief and replace it with truth from God – even when that belief 'feels' true to you.

And that is the hard part: rejecting a belief or a thought that feels true. The question for you to ask in those moments is: who will

I choose to trust? Will I trust my own perceptions and interpretations and understanding? Or will I trust what the Lord has said and what the fruit of the belief or thought reveals about its origins? Through "constant use" (as Hebrews 5:14 states), separating out good from evil through the gift of discernment given to you by the Holy Spirit, and the truth He has written on your heart (Jeremiah 31:33, Hebrews 8:10), you will grow in maturity and wisdom in being able to recognize evil at the onset and reject it straightaway.

Remember, "no lie comes from the truth" (I John 2:21). In the same way, no truth comes from a lie. You can't live with your feet in both camps without getting torn apart. Wisdom says, "Dear friend, do not imitate what is evil but what is good. Anyone who does what is good is from God. Anyone who does what is evil has not seen God" (III John 1:11). Wisdom would lead you to walk in the way of righteousness, because, "The righteousness of the blameless makes their paths straight, but the wicked are brought down by their own wickedness" (Proverbs 11:5): God's built-in system of your consequences coming naturally from your own choices sees to it.

When you live in accordance with the truth of God and reject evil, you will be able to say, "My fruit is better than fine gold; what I yield surpasses choice silver. I walk in the way of righteousness, along the paths of justice, bestowing a rich inheritance on those who love me" (Proverbs 8:19-21). In other words, you will be recognized by your fruit (Matthew 7:16).

Finally, the best way to receive wisdom is to ask for it from God. As James 1:5 says, "If any of you lacks wisdom, you should ask God, who gives generously to all without finding fault, and it will be given to you." A key element to this verse is the statement describing God as giving generously to all without finding fault. So, you are without excuse. Even if you have made myriad mistakes, even if you have sinned repeatedly, even if you have turned your back on God in the past, even if you have been in agreement with the evil one throughout your life, God will not find fault. If you ask, He will give. If you seek, you will find. Wisdom is available, freely given, like all of God's wonderful treasures. All you have to do is ask.

SATAN'S COSTUME JEWELRY

Having identified the source of wisdom as God, and evil's constant warfare against wisdom, how do you recognize the enemy's lies when you are confronted with his strategies? Catching the deception early is crucial to combatting the enemy, because once you are deep in the middle of the enemy's lies, all you can see are the lies. They act like a veil over your eyes, clouding your ability to see anything else. Because the lies 'feel' true, you can be tricked by your own feelings. So, realizing the cunning of the enemy and the kinds of tactics he uses can help prepare you to recognize his deceptions for what they are at the outset.

Satan is the great counterfeiter. He knows God offers you priceless treasures, and he has nothing to offer you that compares. So, he manufactures gems that appear to be of some value, just like a thief might create a counterfeit bauble to replace something valuable he has stolen. He dangles something that mimics God's treasures; for example, he promises hiding yourself behind a mask will protect you from the pain of rejection, thus imitating God's protection. God says to hide in the shadow of His wings (Psalm

17:8), so you confuse hiding yourself with hiding in God, even though the two are vastly different in both motivation and result. Hiding yourself is motivated by fear and doesn't offer any real shielding from rejection, as their words still feel true and still hurt. Hiding in God is motivated in faith. You trust what God says about you, which guards your heart with truth and deflects any lies spoken against you. In getting you to confuse the two, the enemy traps you in a prison of your own making.

Since the enemy is so good at creating counterfeits, you must look deeper than the surface to recognize the quality of what is being offered to you. What does the offering stir as the motive of your heart? Any choice made out of fear is not of God. What is the fruit of the offering? Anything that doesn't match the fruit of the Spirit is not of God. What feeling does the result of the offering produce in you? Anything producing shame is not of God.

Satan's costume jewelry is all made from the same material, the substance of "self" (also known as "the flesh" or "sin nature" in Pauline terms). Self-protection, self-determination, self-judgment, self-aggrandizement, self-debasement, even self-esteem, all arise from a self-centered perspective. They are all counterfeits. Do you see how the treasures of God are mimicked in these examples?

Your identity in Christ is counterfeited as self-esteem, but your own self-evaluation of your worth will always fall well-short of God's view of your true value. In addition, relying on self-esteem forces you to trust your own judgments, which on a very deep level you know are made with partial or flawed information and are therefore suspect. When you compare the counterfeit with the true, you can see how self-esteem pales in the brilliance of God-esteem.

Your God-given authority is undermined by Satan's

counterfeit, self-determination, which attempts to control outcomes that cannot be controlled, leaving you feeling powerless when your attempts to control fail. Anything that smacks of control is from the enemy and of his realm, because God's Kingdom is centered on love, which means it must also include choice, and choice is the antithesis of control.

If you continue to look through the list of treasures of God's Kingdom, you will see the same pattern: what Satan offers instead looks good on the surface but is rotten at its core and produces the opposite of what you desire as it plays out. Watch out for all self-language. God doesn't ask you to rely on yourself; instead, He offers partnership, a sharing of the load through relationship with Him. Satan will tell you it is all up to you and loves to whisper that you are alone. Nothing could be farther from the truth.

Satan also loves to entice you with external, worldly things that gratify the flesh temporarily but produce destruction. He likes to play on your fleshly desire for comfort and ease, offering anything from overindulgence in food to the numbing of drugs and alcohol as methods to achieve the illusion of comfort. He entices you to take the easier path when faced with a choice, hoping you won't evaluate which road is the righteous one but will choose based on ease alone. He encourages you to focus on external measures of your worth, such as your looks or your popularity or your net financial holdings as proof text. In fact, trying to get you to focus a lot of your attention on the things of this world and your circumstances in it is one of his favorite tactics.

However, this worldly setting is just that – a setting in which to share a relationship with Jesus. The circumstances and design of the setting change, but the relationship remains solid and secure and reliable. You will not find true treasures in the things of this world. Instead, you are to live in the Kingdom within you, in the spiritual home He has prepared with you, as Jesus described: "Do not let your hearts be troubled. You believe in God; believe also in me. My Father's house has many rooms; if that were not so, would I have told you that I am going there to prepare a place for you? And if I go and prepare a place for you, I will come back and take you to be with me that you also may be where I am" (John 14:1-3). With Jesus as your partner and first love, you establish your home with Him, and then from this established foundation you are to allow His Kingdom to flow out of you into this world, instead of letting the things of the world flow into you.

WISDOM'S HOUSE

Because of the magnificent treasure of your God-given authority, you get to choose how to build your own internal "house." You decide whether to construct it on your own or alongside the Master Builder. You choose what to use as its foundation. You select the materials with which it will be built. And you decide who resides within it.

A home constructed with the Master Builder will be a house of wisdom. "By wisdom a house is built, and through understanding it is established; through knowledge its rooms are filled with rare and beautiful treasures" (Proverbs 24:3-4). Paul talks about what we choose to build upon the foundation that Christ has laid within our hearts – this foundation of holiness, wholeness, and righteousness through Christ: "For no one can lay any foundation other than the one already laid, which is Jesus Christ. If anyone builds on this foundation using gold, silver, costly stones, wood, hay or straw,

180

their work will be shown for what it is, because the Day will bring it to light. It will be revealed with fire, and the fire will test the quality of each person's work. If what has been built survives, the builder will receive a reward. If it is burned up, the builder will suffer loss but yet will be saved—even though only as one escaping through the flames" (I Corinthians 3:11-15). Do you see once again in these verses how through the system of sowing and reaping/choice and consequence, you choose your own rewards and are responsible for your own results?

It is your choice to pick the materials and manner of your "home" (your spirit). Will you choose precious and costly materials, the cost of which is to give up your self-centered focus, your worldly focus, and your self-directed life? Will you choose what Paul terms "wood, hay, and straw," meaning temporary, common, and cheap materials, the things of the world rather than the Kingdom, things that are easy but not lasting? Notice in these verses Paul warns that what you choose to build will be shown for what it is when the Day of the Lord brings it to light and reveals it with fire. Will what you build now in your spirit survive to remain with you in Heaven, or will it be "burned up" by the Lord's fire? Spiritual maturity is the wisdom to build with the precious materials of the Kingdom.

Jesus told a parable about counting the cost of building prior to taking on the project. "Suppose one of you wants to build a tower. Won't you first sit down and estimate the cost to see if you have enough money to complete it? For if you lay the foundation and are not able to finish it, everyone who sees it will ridicule you, saying, 'This person began to build and wasn't able to finish.'" (Luke 14:28-30). Jesus goes on to say, "In the same way, those of you who do not give up everything you have cannot be my disciples" Luke 14:33).

The temptation presented by the enemy is to hold onto the things of the world you have used in your construction. He fosters pride in what you have built and a belief in needing the so-called security of your own walls to entice you to hold tightly to the worldly things you see as yours. However, Jesus calls on you to know and count the cost of building your home with the wisdom of God as your foundation.

What is the cost of allowing Jesus to design and construct your home? According to Jesus, the cost is giving up everything – letting go of your own perspectives, your reliance on yourself, your beliefs about yourself, about God, and about life, and your judgments. It means letting go of thinking you know. It means releasing your own understanding in exchange for His.

Allowing God to be your Master Builder is a form of death. You must die to everything revolving around and connected with self as god, the original sin of the flesh. Like everything, this type of death can only be done in partnership with Jesus. Any attempt to kill off the sin nature accomplished by the sin nature, by definition, leaves an element of the sin nature behind. You need Jesus to complete the destruction of the sin nature and resurrect you to a new life. Your decision is will you allow Him to finish the work?

Another cost to you is the deep awareness of how foolish you have been. Until you begin to receive some of the wisdom of God, you are able to continue the illusion of the acceptability, even brilliance, of your own so-called wisdom. However, the more wisdom you receive from God, the more your wisdom looks like foolishness. Humility, while a beautiful thing in that it is the recognition you are not God (and don't have to be), is also painful. It's hard to accept how little you know and understand apart from God.

True humility requires a hard, fierce, bold, and unconstrained examination of your own heart. It means seeing your lack, because while you hold some aspects of God's nature in your true identity, you do not have all of God's nature, for you are not God. It means recognizing your deep need. All of these insights, while painful and difficult, are ultimately freeing. You will find true humility is the relief of a terrible burden you have been bearing alone that you were never intended to carry.

Choose, then, consciously and with purpose and intent, how you will build your spiritual house. Select the materials – what you allow to come into your mind and heart and body, what you pursue in your actions and express in your words, what you deem as worthy for your focus – and include those things that will last, choosing wisely what you hold on to and what you put down. Build with the Master Builder as your partner, for whatever you choose to build on Christ's precious foundation will come with you into Heaven. As Paul admonishes, "Therefore, since we have these promises, dear friends, let us purify ourselves from everything that contaminates body and spirit, perfecting holiness out of reverence for God" (II Corinthians 7:1).

CONCLUSION

When you receive the wisdom of God, you are no longer blind, stumbling through life in the darkness. You receive the enlightenment of His Spirit to replace the so-called wisdom of the world, which is foolishness to God. God uses your own mistakes and the natural adversity that comes from living in a sin-infused world to grow His wisdom in you. Through knowing God, you develop reverence for God, which is "the beginning of wisdom," and through His presence He builds the spiritual home, the Kingdom within you. The enemy attempts to entice you with the things of the world, claiming worldly wisdom is easier and safer; however, your battle against the enemy with the truth from God also develops wisdom in you, and Satan's counterfeits begin to look like what they are – cheap imitations of God's treasures.

Although the cost of building wisdom is great, the value of His construction stands the test of the fire of God, and the beautiful results are carried with you into Heaven. Because of God's wisdom, you are:

Free to walk with eyes wide open, seeing clearly the narrow path before you;

Free to reject the enemy's false treasures, recognizing them for the paste they are;

Free to see yourself as God sees you, with wise eyes enlightened by His Spirit;

Free to open your heart up to Jesus completely, holding nothing back, sharing your whole self with Him;

Free to grow in the spiritual maturity His wisdom provides and build your spiritual house from Kingdom materials with Jesus as your Master Builder;

Free to make mistakes and face adversity with strength, knowing Jesus is your Redeemer;

Free to evaluate the cost of Kingdom living, with full knowledge of what you have to gain.

184

Peace comes from receiving wisdom through knowing Christ, having reverence for God, facing adversity, learning from your mistakes, and standing on truth against the enemy's deceptions. Joy comes after paying the cost of dying to self as god, as a strong foundation is established by Christ in love and a beautiful house rises in holiness, filled with the treasures of His Kingdom.

STARTING POINT: QUESTIONS TO EXPLORE WISDOM

Answer the following questions to further explore the wisdom of God. Consider your answers prayerfully and thoughtfully. Don't offer a superficial response and move on to the next question but look deeply within and be as honest with yourself as you can be. Avoid giving "pat" answers you might have heard in church, particularly if you've not examined what those responses mean in depth. These questions are designed to further connect you to His wisdom and help you experience the true freedom that comes from its growth and development within you.

1. Where do you find yourself still walking in blindness, as evidenced by stumbling into unseen obstacles and falling into pits?
2. In what ways have you relied on the wisdom of the world? What have been the consequences of following the wisdom of the world in your life?
3. How has God used your mistakes to grow you in His wisdom?

185

4. How has adversity in your life developed wisdom in you, building perseverance, character, and hope?
5. How could you grow in knowing God in a deeper and more intimate relationship?
6. What embedded lies block your receiving wisdom from God?
7. What counterfeits to Kingdom treasures does the enemy offer you? How can you recognize them?
8. What foundation do you have laid for your spiritual house? What changes do you want to make with Christ in that foundation?
9. What materials have you used to build your spiritual house? What changes do you want to make with Christ in your choice of materials?
10. What cost do you see to allowing Christ to build wisdom in you and to construct your spiritual house of Kingdom materials? What gain do you see?

DESTINATION: PRAYERS FOR WISDOM

Find a quiet place with few distractions to sit with Jesus. Still your mind and quiet your heart by repeating a verse of Scripture meaningful to you; for example, you could repeat, "Wisdom is like honey for you: If you find it, there is a future hope for you, and your hope will not be cut off" (Proverbs 24:14). I have written a prayer for you as an example, but use your own words, from your heart, to ask Jesus to grow you in wisdom: *Lord, you are the source of all wisdom, and you have told me if I ask for wisdom, you will give generously to me. I ask, Jesus, for your wisdom. Bring me new insights from my mistakes. Bring me perseverance from the adversity I face. Help me grow in knowledge of you through the presence of your Spirit. Deepen my reverence and humility. As I open my heart to you, what do you want me to know?*

After you pray, spend time in silent meditation, eyes closed and listening for His answers. He may show you an image in your mind, or you may hear words or phrases in your mind, or you may sense emotions or experiences He brings to you to reveal His wisdom. He also might bring to mind a particular verse or story from Scripture to show you His wisdom. You can recognize responses from the Lord by the peace they stir up in your heart. If an image or word comes to you that brings anxiety or shame, reject it, recenter yourself on Jesus, and ask again. If you think you hear a response that contradicts Scripture, pray against enemy interference, recenter on Jesus, and ask again. Otherwise, don't analyze what comes up or question if it's the Lord. Instead, go with it and follow wherever He takes you. If you are getting "off base," He will let you know. Keep with it, asking Jesus to explain anything you don't understand and to show you more, until you feel He is finished.

If you don't hear anything, don't be concerned or frustrated. Remember, we have an enemy who actively opposes our treasure seeking and tries to thwart our relationship with Jesus. Take a break and come back to your prayer later. This time, if you don't receive a response, ask Jesus what is in the way. It may be a lie you believe, blocking your receipt of His wisdom, such as you are better off following the easy path of self instead of turning to Jesus. You may be unaware you are agreeing with the enemy and your own agreement is getting in your way. Ask Jesus for discernment to identify any "costume jewelry" you may have agreed to accept from the enemy. Whatever Jesus reveals is in the way, ask Him to bring truth to your heart to move the hindrance out of your way. Then return to your prayer request.

Another prayer you could pursue is asking Jesus to develop your discernment. An example of this type of prayer would be: *Lord, I find I am easily confused by the enemy's lies and his attempts to offer me counterfeits to your Kingdom truth. Would you please help me exercise my discernment muscle? Would you provide me with the insights I need to recognize the counterfeits for what they are, and strengthen me to reject them?* A prayer for discernment is a growth process, an ongoing deepening of insight and awareness of enemy tactics and the truth that combats his lies, so continue to pursue discernment, and don't fall into the trap of believing you have "arrived." Satan seeks the tiniest cracks in your home's foundations or walls to slither in, like a cancer, then he latches on and grows in the darkness until his lie has overtaken you. Complacency in spiritual warfare is your enemy.

Finally, you could ask Jesus to work on the construction of your spiritual house. This type of prayer might be: *Lord, I choose you to be my Master Builder. I have tried to build my house on my own for so long, and I'm weary of the effort. I also don't like the results. Would you please show me how you want to build my spiritual home? Show me the cost of the construction and help me to be prepared to let go of everything I now grip so tightly so I might pay the cost. Please reveal to me the materials you will use to build my home. I choose to submit to your design and construction.* Remember to listen as you pray, allowing Jesus to share His processes with you. Dying to self as god is also a growth process, so

188

recognize the grace of God during this process, and offer yourself the same grace, knowing this type of death is hard-fought and hard-won.

As always, remember Jesus is your partner in this endeavor of gaining wisdom. Homes of lasting value are not built overnight. Be patient with yourself in the process. For Jesus, it is the relational aspect of growing your wisdom that matters the most. Deepening your spiritual maturity is a shared process and is accomplished through relationship with Jesus, so keep your focus on connecting with Him and growing in knowing Him more intimately. Allow your reverence for God to intensify. Coming to Him in humility, accepting what you thought of as wisdom is actually foolishness and acknowledging your need, will help you to be more open to receive His treasures.

SETTING THE COURSE: GAINING GOD'S WISDOM

The first section presents concepts you may want to internalize, and the second section lists some actions you may take to apply the information you have studied. Approach the following concepts and actions prayerfully. Avoid any thinking that you must rigidly adhere to them, because these are only suggestions and may not work for you. Everyone is different. Remember, wisdom comes through knowing God, and gaining wisdom isn't up to you alone but is established in partnership with Christ. Use these suggestions to deepen your relationship with Him in your quest to live the Kingdom life.

INTERNALIZE THE CONCEPTS

Consider the implications of your blindness without God's Light and the consequences of continuing to walk in darkness. Contemplate what it would mean and how it would be to walk daily with the light of His insight and wisdom opening your eyes to see.

Meditate on the differences between the wisdom of the world and the wisdom of God. Examine how the wisdom of the world has affected your choices and the consequences you have experienced as a result.

Consider ways your mistakes have been translated into wisdom. Contemplate the adversities you have experienced and seek to see ways you have grown in wisdom through those experiences.

Evaluate the commitment you have had in deepening your relationship with Jesus. Consider ways you may choose to work on this relationship in a purposeful, intentional way.

Consider the enemy's lies you have continued to believe and counterfeit treasures you have continued to seek. Observe how these lies are blocking your receipt of wisdom. Bring the wisdom of God to war against those lies through prayer. Meditate on truth to reject the counterfeit treasures.

Contemplate what it means for Jesus to be the architect, designer, and builder of your spiritual house. Meditate on the foundation He will use to build your home. Examine the materials He will use in its construction. Visualize His hands lovingly

190

building your spiritual home. Consider what it means to share this newly built home with Jesus.

Meditate on the cost of pursuing the wisdom of God. Evaluate your willingness to pay the price of the death of self as god. Consider letting go of everything you have held as your own wisdom (perceptions, knowledge, beliefs, understanding) in exchange for the wisdom of God.

PROCESS THEIR APPLICATION

Keep a wisdom journal where you write down things you learn from your experiences (your mistakes and adversities), things you gain through your conversations with Jesus, insights He gives you as you read and study Scripture, and discernment you learn through the process of spiritual warfare. Review your wisdom writings periodically to ensure you are maintaining growth and development. You can use wisdom already gained to seek additional wisdom by asking Jesus to continue to expound on what He has already revealed and expand your understanding and knowledge.

Make a chart of enemy costume jewelry. In the first column, list the counterfeit offering of the enemy. In the second column, identify the lies associated with the counterfeit jewel. In column three, write out the wisdom offering of God. In the last column, list truths that combat the counterfeit and its lies. Through this process, begin to identify the strategies the enemy typically uses against you. Use this understanding to identify consistent and specific lies you continue to carry embedded in your heart, and take those lies to

Jesus in prayer, asking Him to remove them and replace them with His truth.

Choose a wisdom partner, someone who is also seeking the wisdom of God and who is on a similar path in their spiritual journey. Meet weekly with this individual to discuss new insights gained from God during the week. If your schedule (or theirs) doesn't permit consistent meetings like this, use texts or Skype to share insights and revelations as they come up. Notice any parallels you see in your journeys so you can make connections in those similar, related insights. Become encouragers of each other in the journey toward wisdom and challenge each other to a deeper connection with God.

Spend time in prayer focused specifically on letting go of the so-called wisdom of the world and allowing Jesus to bring self as god in you to its demise. Write down those things of the world you most want to hold onto. One by one, take them to Jesus in prayer. Let Him know you desire to let them go but need His help to release your grip. Listen for His responses. Once you feel ready, carry something that symbolizes what you have released outside your house, have a brief funeral ceremony, and burn it (or throw it in your fireplace if you prefer and the fireplace can accommodate the item).

Conduct a fearless inventory of the state of your spiritual house's foundation, the materials used in its construction, and the items you have used to furnish your spiritual home. With Jesus, tear down anything not of the Kingdom and ask Him to rebuild using Kingdom materials. Keep in mind purging your house, demolition of strongholds, and reconstruction is hard work, so set aside focused, uninterrupted "sacred" time for the job.

SEVEN

The Treasure of Freedom

YOUR COMPASS

Now the Lord is the Spirit, and where the Spirit of the Lord is, there is freedom (II Corinthians 3:17).

The Spirit of the Sovereign LORD is on me, because the LORD has anointed me to proclaim good news to the poor. He has sent me to bind up the brokenhearted, to proclaim freedom for the captives and release from darkness for the prisoners, to proclaim the year of the LORD's favor and the day of vengeance of our God, to comfort all who mourn, and provide for those who grieve in Zion—to bestow on them a crown of beauty instead of ashes, the oil of joy instead of mourning, and a garment of praise instead of a spirit of despair. They will be called oaks of righteousness, a planting of the LORD for the display of his splendor (Isaiah 61:1-3).

For the creation was subjected to frustration, not by its own choice, but by the will of the one who subjected it, in hope that the creation itself will be liberated from its bondage to decay and brought into the freedom and glory of the children of God (Romans 8:20-21).

It is for freedom that Christ has set us free. Stand firm, then, and do not let yourselves be burdened again by a yoke of slavery. You, my brothers and sisters, were called to be free. But do not use your freedom to indulge the flesh; rather, serve one another humbly in love (Galatians 5:1, 13)

Live as free people, but do not use your freedom as a cover-up for evil (I Peter 2:16).

Jesus said, "If you hold to my teaching, you are really my disciples. Then you will know the truth, and the truth will set you free. Very truly I tell you, everyone who sins is a slave to sin. Now a slave has no permanent place in the family, but a son belongs to it forever. So if the Son sets you free, you will be free indeed (John 8:31-32, 34-36).

For we know that our old self was crucified with him so that the body ruled by sin might be done away with, that we should no longer be slaves to sin— because anyone who has died has been set free from sin. For sin shall no longer be your master, because you are not under the law, but under grace. For the wages of sin is death, but the gift of God is eternal life in Christ Jesus our Lord...because through Christ Jesus the law of the Spirit who gives life has set you free from the law of sin and death. The Spirit you received does not make you slaves, so that you live in fear again;

rather, the Spirit you received brought about your adoption to sonship (Romans 6:6-7, 14, 23, 8:2, 15).

In him and through faith in him we may approach God with freedom and confidence (Ephesians 3:12).

MAP KEY: PURCHASING THE FIELD

FREEDOM DEFINED

*Y*ou are free indeed.

Jesus says He has set you free from your indebtedness, your obligation as a result of sin. Where before, all your resources were tied up in trying to secure your freedom, now your debt is paid in full, and you are no longer enslaved to sin. Your resources are available to you for purchasing the field in which the Kingdom treasure lies, ready for you to claim. But what does it mean to be set free?

Freedom is best defined as the right to choose without hindrance or restraint, absent any subjugation, imprisonment, or enslavement. Freedom includes the unimpeded expression of your true identity, without interference. Freedom includes the unrestricted expression of your authority, fully expressed at all times through your choices. The indwelling of the Spirit of God is made possible by your God-given freedom to choose Him. Your sanctification is the result of Jesus setting you free from bondage to

195

sin. In fact, all the treasures of God are tied to the freedom He has provided. Without the freedom to "purchase the field," the treasures of the Kingdom would be lost to you.

Think of sin like a mob boss. You have borrowed huge amounts at exorbitant interest. You can't keep up with the interest payments, much less pay off the debt you owe, and if you don't pay it off, he is going to kill you. So, you are enslaved to this mob boss as long as the debt remains…unless someone else comes along who is willing and able to pay off your debt. It has to be someone who owes nothing to the mob boss, because if he owes a debt, his payment would go toward his own debt. Jesus is that someone. He has never taken from the mob boss and owes no debt, so He is able and willing to pay your debt off completely. He has made restitution to the mob boss on your behalf, and your debt is now paid in full. The mob boss has no more strings to pull, no more demands he can make, nothing else he can hold against you, because your debt is already paid. You are done with him.

Sin is also a kidnapper who has stolen you away in the darkness and held you for ransom. The ransom he demands for your release is unpayable, so he holds you hostage until death. So, Jesus presents himself to the kidnapper as a more valuable hostage and offers to take your place, which the kidnapper accepts, thinking he has gained the power of death over Jesus. Jesus ransomed you out of the hands of the kidnapper with His own life. Of course, the kidnapper didn't know Jesus was also going to escape from death, and through His resurrection redeem you once and for all, so the kidnapper can't ever steal you again, or kill you because the ransom was not paid.

Jesus has bound up Satan, the kidnapper/mob boss. He holds the keys to his chains. Now, the only weapon he has against you is deception – attempts to convince you that you are not in fact free. He tries to manipulate you into binding yourself once again into slavery to sin, so he can usurp your authority and claim power over you once more.

Using fear based on your experiences, he tries to trick you into putting yourself in a prison of your own making, a hiding place he claims is safer than your freedom. He promises bad things will happen if you remain truly free, because you will not be in control, then he offers you the illusion of control in freedom's place, in the form of the lie belief you can determine outcomes and make others act according to your will. And when your attempts to control fail, as they must, he stirs up more fear, calls you a failure, then prompts you to try even more control, creating an ever-descending destructive cycle of fear feeding control feeding fear.

Satan also tries to challenge your identity, the aspects of God's nature created into you. He lies about who you are, using past sins as some sort of measure of identity, while also claiming the feedback of others is more valid than what God says about you. He will even use others' sins against you as proof you are unworthy, unloved, or not measuring up, saying things like, "if they loved you, they wouldn't have done that" or "if they saw you as good enough, they wouldn't treat you that way."

Satan likes to try to bind you back to sin by getting you to focus on the past. He will go over and over things you did, fostering shame and regret and claiming your past defines you. He prompts you to wish things were different, as if the past can be changed. Using phrases like "if only" and "what if," he fuels hopelessness

197

and bitterness in your heart, stealing any joy in the present from you. He also likes to get you to worry about the future, using the past as a barometer of things you "might" do or what "could" happen, once again stealing all your joy from the present.

Perhaps the most dangerous lie of all is their claim that Jesus is to blame for your suffering – that He brought the suffering upon you, or that He should've prevented the bad thing from happening and you from failing, or that He isn't enough to make up for your sins. Being the accuser (Revelation 12:10), he blames everyone but himself for the state of this world. He accuses and shames you for your past mistakes, even though they are wiped away and forgotten. He accuses and shames you for your present sins, even though they are already covered by Jesus' blood payment. He accuses and blames Jesus, both for causing and for not preventing every bad thing that has ever happened to you. The only entity left off Satan's list of blame and shame is himself, but since everything he says is a lie, you can know he is the one responsible.

If Satan's only weapon is lies, then the truth becomes vital to living in your freedom. Jesus said, "If you hold to my teaching, you are really my disciples. Then you will know the truth, and the truth will set you free" (John 8:31-32). To love the truth is to love Jesus, because Jesus is the truth (John 14:6).

According to Jesus, His truth brings freedom. The word, "truth," is mentioned over 100 times in the New Testament alone. Jesus overtly stated, over and over again, "I tell you the truth" as He was teaching a new idea or Kingdom concept. Truth and freedom are inextricably bound together, and you cannot have one without the other. The "belt of truth" is the first weapon mentioned in the armor of God, and it is the one item that holds all other weapons in place (Ephesians 6:14). All of these things let you know that truth is highly valued in the Kingdom.

The truth is, because the mobster/kidnapper is bound and the debt/ransom of sin has been fully covered, you are truly free: free from fear and shame and blame; free to love and to be loved for who you are; free to embrace the truth and reject Satan's deceptions; free from the past and free from worry about the future. You are free to choose Jesus, to love Him with your whole being, and to follow Him as He lives within you.

Jesus came specifically to provide your freedom. In his letter to the Galatians, Paul wrote, "It is for freedom that Christ has set us free" (Galatians 5:1). However, this concept is one that believers have struggled with since before Paul first wrote this letter. Like the Galatians, who believed freedom must be dangerous because they assumed it meant license to do whatever they wanted, Christians today assume there must be expectations, and restrictions and limitations on that freedom, or else…well, who knows what would come from it? Anarchy? Chaos? Licentiousness?

Yet, there it stands – "it is for freedom that Christ has set us free." It doesn't say Christ has set us free except for…it doesn't say He set us free, but…it doesn't claim partial freedom, or freedom in this way but not that. It says it is for freedom that He has set you free. That means, through Christ, you have the right to choose without restraint, hindrance, limitation, or restriction; in other words, you are no longer a slave to the law.

THE LAW VS. GRACE

In Galatians 5, Paul confronts the opposition between the law and grace and asks the question, are you justified by the law or by Christ? According to Paul, righteousness only comes through the

Spirit (Galatians 5:5), and the only thing that counts is faith expressing itself through love (Galatians 5:6). "You who are trying to be justified by the law have been alienated from Christ; you have fallen away from grace" (Galatians 5:4). This is no small thing Paul is saying – you cannot hedge your bets; in other words, you cannot have it both ways. The temptation in the Garden is repeatedly presented to you just like in Eden. Adam and Eve's temptation is the same deception you face each day: "Will I try to create my own salvation by pursuing following the law as my justification?"

The sin nature within you is at war with the Spirit. Paul fought the same battle: "I do not understand what I do. For what I want to do I do not do, but what I hate I do" (Romans 7:15). But Paul stood on the truth that only the cross of Christ can save, and the cross is sufficient to save. The cross, a stumbling block to the Jews and foolishness to the Gentiles (I Corinthians 1:23), is all that matters. This truth is such a critical underpinning of faith that Paul talks about being "cut in on" in the race by any other belief (Galatians 5:7). Paul deemed it so important that this deception be seen for what it is that he even wishes those perverting the gospel and misleading the people back under slavery to the law would "emasculate" themselves (spoken in the context of circumcision in Galatians 5:12), thereby removing their position as men, their power, and their ability to persuade.

Paul also points out that a little yeast (one deception) works its way through the whole batch of dough (Galatians 5:9). Your sin nature is easily swayed to cling to your self-justification through your actions, and along the same lines, you are quick to condemn yourself for falling short of the law, as if those mistakes can undo the cross and remove you from grace. No! According to Paul,

200

binding yourself to the law alienates you from Christ and pulls you away from the loving arms of His grace. How, then, are you to choose your behaviors? Does that mean you should "go on sinning so that grace may increase" (Romans 6:1)?

As Paul says, "By no means! We are those who have died to sin; how can we live in it any longer?" (Romans 6:2). But it isn't the law that keeps you from sinning; instead, the law only identifies what is sin. According to Paul, the entire law is summed up in love (Galatians 5:14), and you are to walk by the Spirit (Galatians 5:16). What does that mean? It means love and the Spirit are to direct your path, not the law.

So, if you ask Jesus what the loving thing to do is in each circumstance and with each choice, and you listen to His Spirit and follow the Spirit's lead with how you choose, what you do, and where you go, you are walking by love and the Spirit. You are not to take Scripture as another list of rules to follow, as the Galatians did, because the deception of Eden continues to distort your perception. Galatians 5:18 is clear: "if you are led by the Spirit, you are not under the law."

Paul is saying the Spirit is opposed to the flesh, and if you are living by the Spirit, your desires will be contrary to the desires of the sin nature. "Those who live according to the flesh have their minds set on what the flesh desires; but those who live in accordance with the Spirit have their minds set on what the Spirit desires. The mind governed by the flesh is death, but the mind governed by the Spirit is life and peace" (Romans 8:5-6). To live in freedom is to accept the leadership of the Spirit within you and to follow the desires of your true heart.

FOLLOWING YOUR TRUE HEART

Paul makes it clear there is a war going on within you between your spirit and the imposition of the sin nature. Think of the sin nature as an overlay of a kind of veil that covers, blurs, and distorts your ability to see the true heart within you, meaning what your spirit desires. The things of the flesh pull on you, distorting your understanding of what you really want to choose. The veil turns you toward selfishness in the expression of your desires and tries to turn you away from love.

But in your true heart, the place where the Spirit of the Living God resides, in the Kingdom within you, love reigns. According to Paul, "Those who belong to Christ Jesus have crucified the flesh with its passions and desires" (Galatians 5:24). When you are able to follow your true heart, you become more like Christ, and you choose based on love. As II Corinthians 3:16-18 explains, "But whenever anyone turns to the Lord, the veil is taken away. Now the Lord is the Spirit, and where the Spirit of the Lord is, there is freedom. And we all, who with unveiled faces contemplate the Lord's glory, are being transformed into his image with ever-increasing glory, which comes from the Lord, who is the Spirit."

Even in following your true heart, self as god, the sin of Eden, presents a temptation: to try in your own strength to crucify the flesh and through your own vision to see and follow the desires of your true heart. If you try to follow your true heart in your own strength, you will fall prey to self-reliance, and you, too, will be "cut in on" in the race and kept from following the truth. In doing so, you make yourself once again a slave to the law, because the only way you can resist the flesh on your own is by desperately trying to follow the law. And you will fail.

You are truly free from the law because the law has been fulfilled in Christ, not because you have followed the law. Your sins (past, present, and future) are already paid for and forgiven. If you follow God's instruction in the law, it is because you know His instructions are for your good, for your protection, for your benefit, and for your well-being – not because you fear God's judgment or feel you must follow the law to be saved. "'I have the right to do anything,' you say—but not everything is beneficial. 'I have the right to do anything'—but not everything is constructive…whatever you do, do it all for the glory of God" (I Corinthians 10:23, 31).

In that way, your true heart's desires inform your choices. Loving God is not something you do; it is the state of being of your true heart. You choose to love God with all your heart because your true heart does love Him. You choose to love yourself because you know how much He loves you. You choose to love your neighbor as yourself because His love has permeated your heart and overflows into others.

Actions motivated by fear are limited to the presence of some punishment, an external source of control. Choices motivated by love are truly free. When you allow your true heart to flow freely from within you, the presence of His Spirit in your heart is witnessed by those around you. By living from your true heart, the law is rendered irrelevant. Why do you need the law if love and the Spirit are leading you? Your true heart desires to walk with His Spirit as a simple byproduct of your love for Jesus.

Walking with the Spirit means partnership with Jesus in everything you do – keeping in step with each other, moving in concert, side by side through every moment of every day of your life. When you walk with the Spirit, the fruit of His presence will be in evidence as He guides your steps. "But the fruit of the Spirit is love, joy, peace, forbearance, kindness, goodness, faithfulness, gentleness and self-control. Against such things there is no law. Since we live by the Spirit, let us keep in step with the Spirit." (Galatians 5:22-23, 25).

How can you tell if you are living from your true heart? Paul instructs you to "test" your actions (Galatians 6:4, II Corinthians 13:5). How do you test your own actions? You cannot examine your actions externally by comparing yourself to others (Galatians 6:4) or by trying to live up to external expectations (I Thessalonians 2:4), but only by evaluating your own motivations by the Spirit.

Testing if you are living by your true heart is an internal rather than an external evaluation. Look beyond your external behavior, which can be deceiving, and check the motives behind that behavior. Look within. Ask the question, "What am I seeking and why am I seeking it?" This type of testing requires an honest and fearless examination of your heartfelt motivations under the revealing light of God's presence within you.

These are the questions of the motivation in your heart: are you motivated by the Spirit and what the Spirit desires or by your sin nature and what the flesh desires? Do you want to follow His Spirit, or do you lust after the ways of this world? Have you searched the Spirit and in humility sought to know His will, or are you following the self and in pride trusting your own understanding? Do you seek control, or do you desire to surrender your will to God's? Honest answers to these questions will reveal the motives of your heart and test your actions.

When you boast to yourself or seek the approval of others for your accomplishments and successes, such as making sure others see you in church or know about your acts of service – when you feel proud of any of your "Christian" behavior, beware lest you become like those Paul says are trying to "impress people by means of the flesh" (Galatians 6:12). Only in the cross of Christ, which has crucified the world to you and you to the world, is the sin nature overcome, and only in the cross can you boast (Galatians 6:14).

What matters in the Kingdom is *becoming* a new creation, being transformed into the likeness of Christ by His presence in your heart. Oneness with Christ is the one true motivation of the true heart, and the only true test of your actions. "Do not conform to the pattern of this world but be transformed by the renewing of your mind. Then you will be able to test and approve what God's will is—his good, pleasing and perfect will" (Romans 12:2).

A CHILD OF GOD

Jesus said, "Very truly I tell you, everyone who sins is a slave to sin. Now a slave has no permanent place in the family, but a son belongs to it forever. So, if the Son sets you free, you will be free indeed" (John 8:34-36). To love Jesus is to be a child of God. "For those who are led by the Spirit of God are the children of God. The Spirit himself testifies with our spirit that we are God's children" (Romans 8:14,16).

As Paul explains, Jesus came "to redeem those under the law, that we might receive adoption to sonship. Because you are his sons, God sent the Spirit of his Son into our hearts, the Spirit who calls out, '*Abba*, Father.' So you are no longer a slave, but God's child; and since you are his child, God has made you also an heir" (Galatians 4:5-7). You are now an heir of God, co-heir with Christ (Romans 8:17). What an astounding truth! You stand beside Christ as the son or daughter of God, just as He is the Son of God, a co-heir, receiving the full inheritance and freedom of a child. You are no longer a slave. You hold a permanent place in God's family.

Who is more valued in a loving family than a child? Who is more precious, more esteemed, or more loved than a son or daughter? A good and loving Father sees, knows, and loves without limits His precious child. No matter what that child might do, the loving Father continues to love. Jesus shared the parable of the prodigal son (Luke 15:11-32) to reveal to His disciples the gracious, merciful, and boundless love of the Father, who received the wayward son back without hesitation and restored his honored position of sonship.

You have been given that honored position, and your inheritance, the Kingdom of God, is guaranteed. "When you believed, you were marked in him with a seal, the promised Holy Spirit, who is a deposit guaranteeing our inheritance until the redemption of those who are God's possession" (Ephesians 1:13-14). All the rights, privileges, and rewards of sonship are yours, given freely by Christ.

What does the son or daughter of a good and loving Father do? Like the example set by Jesus with His Father, they do what they see the Father doing (John 5:19). They desire to spend time with their Father, receiving His love, affection, and attention. They listen to their Father's guidance and instruction, and they want His help. They respect His words and value the wisdom He shares with them. They follow His teaching and His leading. They adopt His values, and they value His truth.

THE TRUTH AND FREEDOM

As mentioned, lies and deceptions are the only remaining weapons of the enemy, and they are what he uses to try to bind you back into slavery, even though you have been set free. When you listen to and buy into the enemy's deceptions, and when you still hold onto lie beliefs, you are inviting Satan to steal your freedom and reinstitute your status as a slave instead of God's child. So, to live fully in the freedom provided by Christ, you must love the truth as your Father loves the truth.

When it comes down to it, do you value truth more highly than you value the things of this world? Do you follow Christ's truth or are you "infants, tossed back and forth by the waves, and blown here and there by every wind of teaching and by the cunning and craftiness of people in their deceitful scheming" (Ephesians 4:14)? When the enemy whispers his lies, do you accept them because they feel true to you, or do you reject it because you know and choose to live by Christ's truth?

Living in the truth requires three elements: 1) loving Jesus with your whole heart; 2) partnering with Jesus through prayer so He can remind you of truth and guide you when you need help; 3) being vigilant and persevering in spiritual warfare. If you love Jesus with your whole heart, you will, by definition, be passionate for the truth. Jesus told me once He wanted me to "eat, sleep, live, and breathe the truth." To me, He meant He wanted me to be zealous for the truth, permeated by it, and absorbed with embracing it at all times.

The second element, listening to and partnering with Jesus, gives you ready access to the truth in any circumstance and prevents you from falling into the pitfall of self-sufficiency and self-determination. At any time, you can ask Jesus the simple question,

"What is the truth?" You are never left to sort out truth from lie on your own. Your role in the partnership is listening and being willing to receive.

The final element, spiritual warfare. is mainly about recognition that you are in a battle, that you have an enemy, and that his weapon, deception, while cunning, cannot defeat you as long as you remain in the truth. When you view lie beliefs as the actual poison that they are, you will be diligent and persevering in embracing truth in all things and at all times.

Satan likes to present perversions and distortions of the truth of Christ, and his distortions of the truth can hinder your experience of your freedom in Christ. The enemy's distortions are often just slight twists or perversions of the truth, presenting beliefs that seem true, and may even sound "Christian," but are one degree off center. Rather than blatant falsehoods, like God doesn't exist (although Satan will certainly pull those obvious lies out of his hat if he can get away with it), his subtle, cunning lies, the ones that are just a slight distortion, are the most dangerous to believers. At the root, most of these perversions take the form of challenging your freedom and trying to bind you once again to the law.

In Galatians 1:6-7, Paul reports being "astonished" at the people of Galatia, who less than a year prior so openly accepted the good news he presented to them about the grace of Christ and the freedom that grace affords but have now accepted "a different gospel – which is really no gospel at all." He identifies the reason for their confusion as a perversion of the gospel of Christ. This perversion Paul references is the belief that something more than grace is required for salvation. I call this perversion the "plus X" belief. Yes, you have been given grace by Christ, but you also need something more – grace plus (fill in the blank) – to be saved. In Paul's time, it was grace plus circumcision. Translated into present day language, this means grace plus you must follow the law.

In the current time, the plus X belief takes different forms. Perhaps it is tithing, or attending church, or serving in the church, or not committing certain specific sins, but the bottom line is, something more is required for your salvation. The cross of Christ is not enough. Certainly, tithing, church attendance, service, etc., are all good things, but adding them on as a requirement for salvation is a perversion of the gospel. If you have a plus X belief, you are demeaning Christ's great sacrifice as insufficient to accomplish what He set out to do, and you are leaving it up to you to accomplish acceptability, which means it is doomed to fail. Self as god is at work in all plus X beliefs, because you are trying to be your own savior.

Here are some suggestions of ways to identify when you are not living in true freedom:

1. Should's – when you hear yourself saying what you "should" or "shouldn't" be doing or "should've" or "shouldn't have" done, you have bought into the enemy's lie of shame and condemnation, and in so doing you have bound yourself back to the Law and under the yoke of its slavery (Romans 8:1, Galatians 2:19-21).

2. Have to's – when you hear yourself using the language, "have to," you have bought into the enemy's lie of fear (because have to's are an attempt to exert control over outcomes), and once again, you have bound yourself to the yoke of slavery to control (Romans 6:14, Romans 7:6).

3. Can'ts – when you hear yourself saying "I can't," you have bought into the enemy's lie of victimization, you have abdicated your God-given authority and responsibility for your choices, and you have bound yourself under the yoke of slavery to Satan's usurped authority. (Philippians 4:13, Mark 10:27).

4. Enough's – when you notice yourself asking if you are good enough, if you have done enough, if you are smart enough or talented enough, any "enough" judgment, you have bought into the enemy's lie of measuring up and bound yourself under the yoke of judgment (Romans 3:21-22, Romans 4:14, Philippians 3:9).

Instead of the should's, have to's, can'ts, and enough's, you have been given "want to" and "choose to" by God as replacements. These phrases are verbal expressions of the truth of your freedom.

PARTNERSHIP IN FREEDOM

Jesus uses the analogy of a vine and branches to describe partnering with Him. He says, "Remain in me, as I also remain in you. No branch can bear fruit by itself; it must remain in the vine. Neither can you bear fruit unless you remain in me" (John 15:4). You might read this description and feel it sounds more like captivity than freedom, to remain in Jesus as He remains in you, and not bearing fruit alone; however, partnership with Jesus is not a loss of your identity and authority. In fact, the opposite is true: true partnership in freedom is the fulfillment of your identity and authority, freeing you for full expression of who you are and the pursuit of your true heart. Remember, Jesus is the one promised by Isaiah who came to proclaim freedom for the captives (Isaiah 61:1).

210

Sometimes, the way a partnership with Jesus is discussed sounds more like how you would work with a business partner. The business partner is in his office, and you can go check in with him at any time, getting input and feedback on decisions, then you leave and go back to your office to do your work, and he does his.

Partnership with Jesus is not two individuals, each playing their own part toward a common goal. Partnership with Jesus is flowing through life together, moving in concert. You are united, even while each identity is completely valued and respected. You are enveloped in Him, and He dwells in you. Think of a branch on a vine. The branch is a part of the vine, and vice versa. On its own, the branch is fragile and vulnerable, but connected to the vine, the branch is able to grow and thrive. Nutrients flow through the vine's roots into the branches, feeding the growth of the whole plant and producing fruit. A healthy vine means a healthy branch. The vine provides a constant anchor, and the strength of the vine's grounding provides strength for the branch, keeping the branch from blowing away in the wind or being ripped apart by the storm.

In the same way, Jesus is your anchor. He stabilizes you during the storms of life. His truth provides nutrients for your spirit and protection from the disease of enemy lies. Fear and shame that attempt to undermine your experience of freedom can't find purchase in Him, so because of His presence in you and your abiding in Him, the lies lose their ground in you as well. The sins of your past are wiped off the slate and replaced by His grace, and even your mistakes are transformed into good fruit. Through your relationship with Jesus, your identity is realized, your authority is secured, and your freedom is perfected.

CONCLUSION

When Jesus sets you free, you are free indeed. Your captivity of sin is abolished once and for all, and your captor is now the captive. His only remaining weapon of deception only works if you agree to believe it, making him truly powerless against you, as long as you live in the truth. Your enslavement to the law has been replaced by grace, so you are free to follow your true heart, where love reigns, because nothing is needed beyond grace to make you acceptable to God. As God's heir, you are guaranteed the full inheritance of a beloved child. As God's partner, you are anchored in His strength, protected by His truth, and fed by His love.

The cost of your freedom has been paid in full by Jesus on the cross, so nothing can hold you captive. No longer a slave, you are brought into God's family in honor and given a seat at the table of the feast of the King. Because He has ransomed you and paid your debt, you are:

Free to let go of "everything that hinders and the sin that so easily entangles" (Hebrews 12:1);

Free to join with Jesus as partner, becoming one, flowing with Him and moving in concert, while continuing to express your identity in its fullness;

Free to set aside the desires of the flesh and follow your true heart, from the motive of love;

Free to accept grace as enough and refuse to add anything beyond grace as a requirement for salvation and acceptance;

Free to reject the deceptions of the enemy, overcoming his lies in power with the truth of Christ;

212

Free to live without being bound to or restricted by the law, instead following the guidance of the Spirit within you from a heart of desire and love for Jesus;

Free to purchase the field containing all the treasures of the Kingdom of God.

Peace comes from living in oneness with Jesus like a branch anchored in the vine, allowing Him to help you live in the truth and reject the enemy's lies, and knowing His grace is sufficient for you, because His strength in made perfect in your weakness. Joy comes from knowing you are God's child and heir, honored and beloved, rooted and established in His love and filled with the treasures of His Kingdom.

STARTING POINT: QUESTIONS TO EXPLORE FREEDOM

Answer the following questions to further explore the freedom of God. Consider your answers prayerfully and thoughtfully. Don't offer a superficial response and move on to the next question but look deeply within and be as honest with yourself as you can be. Avoid giving "pat" answers you might have heard in church, particularly if you've not examined what those responses mean in depth. These questions are designed to further help you understand and experience His freedom and enjoy the grace of Christ to its fullest.

1. In what ways are you still living as if you are in debt to your sin or captive to it? In what ways is your freedom in Christ expressed in your life today?

2. What deceptions has the enemy used to try to trick you into returning to enslavement to sin?

3. What are some examples in your life where the truth has brought you freedom? What truth do you need to receive from Jesus to experience freedom in those areas still in bondage?

4. What are your "plus X's"? In other words, what have you added to grace to be acceptable and receive salvation and freedom from Jesus?

5. In what ways are you living as if you are still under the governance of the law?

6. What challenges from your flesh do you experience? In other words, what do you battle in your sin nature? How do those challenges hinder your experience of freedom in Christ?

7. In what ways do you see yourself living from your true heart? Where does your true heart need to be released for its full expression?

8. What motivates your actions? What is important enough to you for you to seek it and why are you seeking it?

9. In what ways are you behaving like a child of God? How are you acting as if you are a slave instead of a child?

10. How does freedom make it possible for you to pursue the other treasures of the Kingdom? What ways are you living like a branch attached to the true vine? Where do you need to reconnect to the vine?

DESTINATION: PRAYERS FOR FREEDOM

Find a quiet place with few distractions to sit with Jesus. Still your mind and quiet your heart by repeating a verse of Scripture meaningful to you; for example, you could repeat, "In him and through faith in him we may approach God with freedom and confidence" (Ephesian 3:12). I have written a prayer for you as an example, but use your own words, from your heart, to ask Jesus to grow you in your freedom: *Lord, you say you have set me free, but I still feel like I am in bondage to my sins, both past and present. I ask you, Jesus, to help me experience the freedom your sacrifice has provided. Show me the truth about the cross, your grace, and my release from slavery to my sins. Would you help me to understand the verses about you no longer remembering our sins and how you cast them away as far as the east from the west. As I open my heart to you, what do you want me to understand about the freedom you provide?*

After you pray, spend time in silent meditation, eyes closed and listening for His answers. He may show you an image in your mind, or you may hear words or phrases in your mind, or you may sense emotions or experiences He brings to you to help you experience His freedom. He also might bring to mind a particular verse or story from Scripture to explain freedom and release you from your bondage to enemy lies. You can recognize responses from the Lord by the peace they stir up in your heart. If an image or word comes to you that brings anxiety or shame, reject it, recenter yourself on Jesus, and ask again. If you think you hear a response that contradicts Scripture, pray against enemy interference, recenter on Jesus, and ask again. Otherwise, don't analyze what comes up or question if it's the Lord. Instead, go with it and follow wherever He takes you. If you are getting "off base," He will let you know. Keep with it, asking Jesus to explain anything you don't understand and to show you more, until you feel He is finished.

If you don't hear anything, don't be concerned or frustrated. Remember, we have an enemy who actively opposes our treasure seeking and tries to thwart our relationship with Jesus. Take a break and come back to your prayer later. This time, if you don't receive a response, ask Jesus what is in the way. It may be a lie you believe, blocking your receipt of His freedom, such as if you were really free, you'd be out of control. You may be unaware you are agreeing with the enemy and your own agreement is getting in your way. Ask Jesus for discernment to identify any hindrances to freedom you may have agreed to accept from the enemy. Whatever Jesus reveals is in the way, ask Him to bring truth to your heart to move the hindrance out of your way. Then return to your prayer request.

Another prayer you could pursue involves testing your heart through honest and fearless examination of your motives as revealed in the light of Christ. An example of this type of prayer would be: *Lord, I desire to follow your instructions to test my actions by examining my motives, but I can't do this on my own. I need your help and revelation to see my motives clearly. Would you shine a light on my true heart and reveal my motives? I want to know what I am seeking and why I am seeking it. Help me to see why I do what I do and what I am valuing most according to my choices. Would you please help me make my choices from a motive of love in all things? What would you like to show me about my motives?* The honest evaluation of your motives is an ongoing process of heart examination. The testing of your heart is not a "one and done" type of prayer, but must be pursued on a continual basis, knowing the enemy is relentless in his attempts to pull you out of your true heart and into self as god. It is important to not try to do this examination in your own strength and knowledge, because the sin of Eden always lurks as a temptation of the flesh. Rely on Jesus to reveal your motives to you through listening for His responses to your prayer.

Finally, you could ask Jesus to anchor you in Him and Him in you such that you flow with Him as one and move in concert with Him. This type of prayer might be: *Lord, I know you are the one true vine, an anchor for me, grounding me and strengthening me through the process of being made one with you. I desire to live from my true heart as your partner, but I'm used to acting as if you are more of a business partner who I check in with on occasion for help with decision making and when I'm in trouble. Would you show me what being connected to you like a branch on a vine is like? Would you teach me how to flow with you and move in concert with you through life? Would you help me to accept this level of intimacy with you?* Always remember to listen as you pray and remain open to whatever He wants to show you or wherever He wants to take you. Intimacy at this level can be scary, but He is a good and loving Father who wants only good for you. If you know this, or if He can show you this through prayer, you won't be afraid to open your heart to Him completely.

As always, don't try to figure out the answers yourself. Remember, for Jesus, everything is about the relationship, including your freedom. Love took Him to the cross, love is the reason for the grace in which you live, and love is what motivates His desire to be one with you. So, everything that provides your freedom comes from His love. Allow yourself to experience the height and depth and width and length of His love for you. Through that experience, you will know your freedom.

SETTING THE COURSE: LIVING IN FREEDOM

The first section presents concepts you may want to internalize, and the second section lists some actions you may take to apply the information you have studied. Approach the following concepts and actions prayerfully. Avoid any thinking that you must rigidly adhere to them, because these are only suggestions and may not work for you. Everyone is different. Remember, freedom comes through Christ alone, and living in freedom isn't something you can accomplish but is established through partnership with Christ. Use these suggestions to deepen your relationship with Him in your quest to live the Kingdom life.

INTERNALIZE THE CONCEPTS

Consider the significance of your freedom from indebtedness to sin. Meditate on the kind of love who would pay for this type of freedom at such a high price to Himself.

Consider the significance of your freedom from captivity to sin. Meditate on the kind of love who would give Himself as ransom in exchange for your freedom.

Examine the tactics and deceptions the enemy uses to try to bind you back to slavery to sin. Contemplate truths you can use to fight against the enemy's lies.

218

Meditate on this verse: "For it is by grace you have been saved, through faith—and this is not from yourselves, it is the gift of God" (Ephesians 2:8). Contemplate what it means that His grace is sufficient.

Evaluate how you live from your true heart vs. from your flesh. Examine the motives of your heart behind choices you have made and are making. Consider how love as a motive might change your choices.

Meditate on your position as heir of God and co-heir with Christ. Contemplate the significance of this declaration. Evaluate the impact of being a child of God on your day-to-day life.

Visualize Christ in you and you in Him. Experience the flow of shared love between you. Bring yourself in alignment with Him, moving as you see Him moving. Meditate on the advantages of remaining in the vine as opposed to going it on your own.

Process their Application

Make a collage of sins from your past. You can use pictures, drawings, cut-outs, or symbols to represent those sins. Once the collage is completed, take it outside to a fire pit or stand before a fireplace and put your collage into the fire. Watch while the flames consume the representation of your sins. As the fire burns the paper to ash, pray and thank Jesus for consuming your sins in His holy fire. Once the paper is completely gone, brush your hands together, turn, and intentionally walk away from the fire, saying, "Remembered no more."

219

In prayer, choose a truth you received from Jesus you know in your heart is true, meaning it feels true in your heart and you are certain it is true in your head. This will be your anchoring truth. On your computer, create a meme of this truth. You can print it and post it somewhere prominent in your home, or, if you'd like, you can make it your home screen on your computer. The goal is to have it displayed somewhere you will see it often. Whenever you notice your anchor truth, say it aloud. When you feel anxious, fearful, or ashamed, repeat this truth. Visualize it as an anchor holding you firmly to the solid ground; for example, like the roots of a vine holding you steady in the wind. You can make any number of truth memes and post them various places but have one you consider foundational to you to use as your anchor.

For one day, practice asking the question "What is the loving thing to do?" as you make each decision and respond to each person throughout the day. At the end of the day, journal your experiences, looking at how asking the question influenced or changed your responses. In your journal, explore how you felt as you made each decision and decide if you would like to continue asking the question the next day. If you can ask this question consistently for about 3 weeks, you will develop a habit of automatically asking the question as you make your decisions.

Before you go to bed, review your day, and for each action or response, label it as "flesh" or "spirit," depending on your assessment of what motivated your choice. Count the number of "flesh" answers and the number of "spirit" answers and keep a daily tally. See at the end of the week if you notice any trends in either direction, or if the ratio remains about the same. Just by keeping track, you will be increasing your awareness of the status of your internal battle. Prayerfully ask Jesus for help in moving the battle forward toward the spirit.

Conduct a fearless inventory of your motives, testing your actions by looking at the process behind them. With Jesus, remove any motive not of the Kingdom and ask Him to replace the false motive with a true one. Keep in mind any internal evaluation is hard work, so set aside quiet, uninterrupted, undisturbed prayer time for the process. You must be conscious of your motives before you will ask Jesus to help you change those you do not like and recognize those that do not produce good fruit.

EIGHT

The Treasure of the Kingdom

YOUR COMPASS

I will give you hidden treasures, riches stored in secret places, so that you may know that I am the LORD, the God of Israel, who summons you by name (Isaiah 45:3).

Do not store up for yourselves treasures on earth, where moths and vermin destroy, and where thieves break in and steal. But store up for yourselves treasures in heaven, where moths and vermin do not destroy, and where thieves do not break in and steal. For where your treasure is, there your heart will be also (Matthew 6:19-21).

This is what the kingdom of God is like. A man scatters seed on the ground. Night and day, whether he sleeps or gets up, the seed sprouts and grows, though he does not know how. All by itself the soil produces grain—first the stalk, then the head, then the full kernel in the head. As soon as the grain is ripe, he puts the sickle to it, because the harvest has come (Mark 4:26-29).

Once, on being asked by the Pharisees when the kingdom of God would come, Jesus replied, "The coming of the kingdom of God is not something that can be observed, nor will people say, 'Here it is,' or 'There it is,' because the kingdom of God is in your midst." (Luke 17:20-21).

"Listen! A farmer went out to sow his seed. As he was scattering the seed, some fell along the path, and the birds came and ate it up. Some fell on rocky places, where it did not have much soil. It sprang up quickly, because the soil was shallow. But when the sun came up, the plants were scorched, and they withered because they had no root. Other seed fell among thorns, which grew up and choked the plants, so that they did not bear grain. Still other seed fell on good soil. It came up, grew and produced a crop, some multiplying thirty, some sixty, some a hundred times." Then Jesus said, "Whoever has ears to hear, let them hear." When he was alone, the Twelve and the others around him asked him about the parables. He told them, "The secret of the kingdom of God has been given to you." (Mark 4:3-11).

Blessed are the poor in spirit, for theirs is the kingdom of heaven. Blessed are the pure in heart, for they will see God. Blessed are the peacemakers, for they will be called children of God. Blessed are those who are persecuted because of righteousness, for theirs is the kingdom of heaven (Matthew 5:3, 8-10).

"Very truly I tell you, no one can see the kingdom of God unless they are born again." "How can someone be born when they are old?" Nicodemus asked. "Surely they cannot enter a second time into their mother's womb to be born!" Jesus answered, "Very truly

224

I tell you, no one can enter the kingdom of God unless they are born of water and the Spirit. Flesh gives birth to flesh, but the Spirit gives birth to spirit. You should not be surprised at my saying, 'You must be born again.' The wind blows wherever it pleases. You hear its sound, but you cannot tell where it comes from or where it is going. So it is with everyone born of the Spirit." (John 3:3-8).

No one who puts a hand to the plow and looks back is fit for service in the kingdom of God (Luke 9:62).

Your kingdom come, your will be done, on earth as it is in heaven (Matthew 6:10).

Map Key: Pearls of the Kingdom

The Kingdom Defined

*Y*ou live in the Kingdom of God.

Your eternal life has already begun. In your spirit, you have sold everything to purchase the pearls of highest value. His Kingdom exists within you (Luke 17:20-21) and flows out of you into this world.

You may wonder, then, why there is still so much pain and suffering, and why tears and grief and anguish are still a part of your life, since Scripture promises Jesus "will wipe every tear from their eyes. There will be no more death or mourning or crying or pain, for

225

the old order of things has passed away (Revelation 21:4). It is certainly true the old order has passed away within your spirit, for the Holy Spirit lives in you, which means you "are being transformed into His image with ever-increasing glory" (II Corinthians 3:18), and "you were washed, you were sanctified, you were justified in the name of the Lord Jesus Christ and by the Spirit of our God" (I Corinthians 6:11). However, your spirit is encased within your flesh, and your flesh continues to be connected to this world, which is still "groaning as in the pains of childbirth right up to the present time" (Romans 8:22). The world has not yet been "swallowed up by life" (II Corinthians 5:4). In fact, according to Jesus, "the kingdom of heaven has been subjected to violence, and violent people have been raiding it" (Matthew 11:12). This is why suffering, pain, and death continue to hold sway in this world.

C. S. Lewis described it this way: "Enemy-occupied territory – that is what this world is. Christianity is the story of how the rightful king has landed, you might say landed in disguise, and is calling us to take part in a great campaign of sabotage."[2] You are a spy behind enemy lines, bringing the Kingdom of God into enemy-occupied territory. You are part of His invading force, and your calling, your assignment for the Kingdom, is to usher the Kingdom into this world. What is this Kingdom you are tasked with bringing to the world?

A kingdom is best defined as a domain ruled by a king, but God's Kingdom is a spiritual domain where the sovereignty of God and Christ extends, whether in heaven or on earth; in other words, where God reigns in authority. The Kingdom of God is also defined as the realm in which God's will is fulfilled. So, since God reigns in authority in you, His sovereignty extends over you, and as you pray for and seek His will to be done, you are a Kingdom carrier.

Jesus taught a parable He said reveals the secret of the Kingdom (Mark 4:11). The parable of the sower (Mark 4:3-11) is one of the few parables Jesus explained. About this parable, he said, "Don't you understand this parable? Then how will you understand any parable?" (Mark 4:13). In other words, this parable contains the secret to understanding all His other parables. By unpacking this parable, you will be given the keys to understanding His Kingdom.

The parable of the sower is divided into three parts: the parable itself, Jesus' commentary on the secret of the Kingdom, and the parable's explanation. Jesus uses the analogy of planting because people at that time would've readily understood how planting seeds works and the amount of tending it takes to produce fruit. In this parable, He begins to reveal the secret of the Kingdom. The secret of the Kingdom of God must be revealed, because you cannot perceive it or understand it as long as you are outside the Kingdom.

Immediately before this section of Mark, Jesus describes who is inside and who is outside the Kingdom (Mark 3:31-35). Those inside the Kingdom are those who recognize Jesus for who He is and do God's will, which is to be in relationship with Him. Therefore, the secret of the kingdom of God must be understood against the backdrop of Jesus' person – who He is. In Him, the Kingdom of God has come into the world, and the secret of the Kingdom is being in relationship with Jesus.

So, in this parable, the sower of the seed is Jesus. What seed did He come to sow? In His explanation of the parable, Jesus references logos (which is translated, word): "The sower sows the word" (Mark 4:14). He isn't referring to the Bible here. Logos in Greek refers to universal divine reason, transcending all opposing forces and imperfections in creation and in humanity. Logos is the eternal and unchanging truth present from the time of creation. John 1:1 says the Logos was from the beginning, was with God, and was God. Then, in John 1:14, it says the Logos was made flesh and made His dwelling with humankind.

Jesus is the unifying and liberating revelatory force which reconciles the human with the divine, available to every individual who seeks it. In other word, Jesus made it possible for you to be one with God. The seed He sows is Himself.

Next, Jesus explains the seed is sown within four different kinds of hearts. The first heart He calls the path. Jesus explains this type of heart this way: Jesus lands on the heart, but Satan (represented in the parable by birds) immediately comes and snatches the seed away. This kind of heart may be well-worn, indecisive, uncommitted, indifferent, and dry and packed down, as someone who shoves their heart down deep and hidden, disconnected and ignored.

The second heart He describes as rocky ground. Jesus explains this type of heart this way: the heart receives Jesus with joy, but the seed doesn't take root, so when trouble or persecution comes, any growth withers and falls away. This kind of heart might be hardened, cynical, shallow, inflexible, stubborn, fearful, and self-protected.

Jesus explains the seed in the third heart is sown among thorns or weeds. Jesus explains this heart this way: other things choke out Jesus and the seed produces no fruit. This kind of heart might be filled with lies, worldly in its focus, controlling, manipulative, and focused on self as god and on fulfilling selfish desires.

The fourth heart is described as good soil. Jesus explains this heart this way: very simply, they hear and receive Jesus. This type of heart bears good fruit in varying amounts, because of receiving Jesus. When the word is presented, this heart might be open, willing, softened, flexible, receptive, warm, humble, and all-in, so the seed takes root, grows, and blossoms. The secret of the Kingdom revealed in this parable is Jesus, who has come to you to unite you with God. He offers Himself to your heart, like seed planted to bear fruit. Those inside the Kingdom of God are those who receive Him and bear fruit.

Your heart can at any time become a dry path, rocky ground, or weed-choked. You need to tend your heart, so the enemy doesn't snatch your experience of Jesus' presence away, times of difficulty don't wither you. so you fall away, or lies don't choke Jesus' truth out of your heart.

Tending your Heart

Scripture says Jesus goes before you to prepare your Kingdom home (John 14:2), which means He is the one who prepares your heart to receive Him, since your heart is His home. Like everything, tending the ground of your heart is done in partnership. On your own, you are unaware of the hardness of your soil or the deep-rooted weeds that grow there, but with His help, your ground can be plowed and readied to grow the fruit of His Kingdom within you.

First, your hidden, disconnected, deadened heart must be brought up from the depths and out of its hiding place and brought back to life. Scripture says you have made a covenant with death, and "have made a lie (your) refuge and falsehood (your) hiding place" (Isaiah 28:15) in an attempt to provide your own protection and maintain your illusion of control. In response, God says He has given you "a precious cornerstone for a sure foundation" (Isaiah 28:16) for your house, and this cornerstone, who is Jesus, will "sweep away your refuge, the lie, and water will overflow your hiding place," and "your covenant with death will be annulled" (Isaiah 28:17-18).

He goes on to say, "When a farmer plows for planting, does he plow continually? Does he keep on breaking up and working the soil?" (Isaiah 28:24). The answer, of course, is no, once the ground is plowed planting begins. Your heart is handled in the same way. Jesus brings your hidden and disconnected heart out of its hiding place, which may be a painful and difficult process. But the plowing process doesn't go on forever. He restores your heart to life, and plants His good seed, Himself, in the newly tilled soil to produce a good crop.

Breaking up your soil requires your willingness to allow Jesus to connect you to your true self. If the pain and difficulty of this worldly life has prompted you to bury your heart to protect yourself from those feelings, you may resist the invitation from Jesus to come out of hiding, fearing experiencing pain, and you might be right that reconnecting to your heart may be painful initially, in the same way going to the doctor to cut out an abscess is painful. But you wouldn't leave the infection in you to avoid the pain of the surgery. Pain is temporary; healing is lasting.

His plowing process begins with a personal revelation of who He is. To see your true self, which is a reflection of aspects of

His nature, you must first know the truth of His nature. Once false perceptions of His character are addressed and you come to know Him better, Jesus begins to remind you of your identity and reconnect you to your true self. As part of this process, Jesus reveals how He sees you and His deep love for you. Paul's prayer for you "to grasp how wide and long and high and deep is the love of Christ, and to know this love that surpasses knowledge—that you may be filled to the measure of all the fullness of God" (Ephesians 3:18-19) was because he personally experienced the healing power of truly knowing the extent of God's unsurpassed love for you.

Next, Jesus prepares your hardened, shallow heart for the trouble and persecution that is certain to come. To prepare you, the Lord strengthens you and disciplines you to help you stand when difficulty comes (Deuteronomy 8:5, Psalm 89:21, Isaiah 35:3). Once again, this process may be painful. Digging up rocks is labor-intensive and cuts deeply into the soil. Through this "strict training," you are prepared to "run in such a way to win the prize" and "a crown that will last forever" (I Corinthians 9:24-25).

The discipline of God is always loving and never harsh, so you don't need to fear it. Instead, it is more like weight training, building up your spiritual muscles. Through diving into Scripture with the guidance of the Holy Spirit, practicing spiritual disciplines, developing your relationship with Jesus through constant prayer, and allowing the love you receive from Him to flow out to others, not as a requirement or structured ritual but from a heart of desiring to know God, you are strengthened with deeply-rooted truth to stand when adversity comes your way or the enemy comes against you.

In addition, Jesus uses the hardship that comes to you in this world to build you up and strengthen you. Remember, Jesus doesn't create or cause the hardship; the trouble comes from the sin still infesting the world and the enemy who is still at war with God on this plane, just as Jesus said it would (John 16:33). Everyone experiences difficulty to varying degrees, and everyone will eventually experience at least one crushing, excruciating suffering, like the loss of a loved one or a trauma of some kind, because death still holds sway in the flesh. But He takes all the hardship, even death, and redeems it by using it to work in you for your good (Romans 8:28). James described it this way: "Consider it pure joy, my brothers and sisters, whenever you face trials of many kinds, because you know that the testing of your faith produces perseverance. Let perseverance finish its work so that you may be mature and complete, not lacking anything" (James 1:2-4).

So, through the normal hardships of life in this sinful world, Jesus builds up your perseverance and spiritual maturity. As a result, when the inevitable sting of death comes, you are prepared to face it with strong, mature faith and perseverance. Fear will not cripple you; grief will not lead to hopelessness. As the writer of Hebrews says, "no discipline seems pleasant at the time, but painful. Later on, however, it produces a harvest of righteousness and peace for those who have been trained by it" (Hebrews 12:11). So, you have His promise of a harvest of both righteousness and peace, a worthy yield indeed.

Finally, Jesus pulls out the lies that infest your garden, from fear and shame to self as god, and shifts your focus from the world to the Kingdom. The weeding process involves exposing the lies, digging down to their roots, culling them from your heart, and replacing the lies with truths that fill up the gaps left in your soil.

The first step is exposure through revelation. Once again,

Jesus can use everyday challenges to expose a lie or lies you believe. He might point out your fear-based or shame-based responses to those challenges, He might prompt another believer to counter your belief, or He might confront the lie with truth to reveal its nature. Whatever method He uses to reveal your lies to you, once you see the lie, He takes you through prayer to the place where the lie was first planted. This place could be a single memory, a representative event, or a string of experiences all reinforcing the lie you believe. He goes with you to that place and brings healing for the pain the lie caused and truth to plant in your heart to replace the lie.

The most difficult lie is the sin of Eden, because the self as god lie is so deeply planted, it is almost a part of your DNA. This lie is also extremely enticing, and you may find you are tempted to hold out at least some small corner of your heart to hold as your own, somewhere you can maintain your illusion of control. Be forewarned, however, if the enemy holds even a crack in the foundation of your house (for holding onto self as god in any way is an opening for the enemy), he will continue to push through this crack until it becomes an open doorway he can rush through and overcome you. You will need Christ's help to "count yourselves dead to sin but alive in Christ Jesus" (Romans 6:11).

Thus, the sin of Eden must be crucified with Christ. As Paul describes it: "We are those who have died to sin; how can we live in it any longer? Or don't you know that all of us who were baptized into Christ Jesus were baptized into his death? We were therefore buried with him through baptism into death in order that, just as Christ was raised from the dead through the glory of the Father, we too may live a new life. For if we have been united with him in a death like his, we will certainly also be united with him in a resurrection like his. For we know that our old self was crucified with him so that the body ruled by sin might be done away with, that we should no longer be slaves to sin—because anyone who has died has been set free from sin" (Romans 6:2-7). Your "old self" is the self that believes you can be like God, and it must die for you to be "set free from sin" and filled with "all the fullness of God."

The tending of your heart is not a one-and-done affair; just like in a physical garden, it is an ongoing process of planting and weeding. As a farmer plants various types of seeds for different seasons, Jesus plants in your heart to bear the fruit needed in the different seasons of your life. Your experience of His presence and your living in His Kingdom within you grows and deepens with each planting. But remember, the farmer doesn't "plow continually." When you receive a truth planted in your heart, that truth takes root, your heart is forever changed, and each truth planted bears fruit. You won't have to go back and re-plow that ground.

So, know this: "it is for freedom that Christ has set (you) free" (Galatians 5:1). His work on the cross is a completed work. You have been set free. When you were bound in sin, you "followed the ways of this world and of the ruler of the kingdom of the air, the spirit who is now at work in those who are disobedient…gratifying the cravings of (your) flesh, following its desires and thoughts" (Ephesians 2:2-3). But by His grace, God has resurrected you in Christ, raised you up, and seated you with Jesus in the heavenly realms (Ephesians 2:4-6).

You are no longer of this world, even though you still live in it (John 15:19, 17:16). Because your body remains in this world, you still face the enemy of God and the battles against the flesh, but the presence of Christ within you gives you a haven, a home away from this world. His Spirit and your spirit are united in this Kingdom home. There, Jesus Himself is your peace (Ephesians 2:14, John 16:33), no matter what worldly circumstances come your way, for "the mind governed by the Spirit is life and peace" (Romans 8:6). The world may be the setting in which you live, but the Kingdom of God is your true home.

ESTABLISHING THE KINGDOM WITHIN

Your life in the Kingdom begins with your union with Jesus. "As a young man marries a young woman, so will your Builder marry you; as a bridegroom rejoices over his bride, so will your God rejoice over you" (Isaiah 62:5). Jesus is your Builder, and He becomes one with you in a wedding of spirits. Your bridegroom provides "fine linen, bright and clean" (Revelation 19:8) for you to wear, meaning He cleanses your sin and makes you holy, set apart for Him. This wedding is the start of a life together of sharing love.

Just like relationship deepens and love grows over the life of a marriage, so does your Kingdom life grow and change from its inception until you finally leave this world and return home. Jesus uses two connected parables to describe the growth process that takes place in you following your union with Jesus. The first once again compares the Kingdom to planting a seed: "The kingdom of heaven is like a mustard seed, which a man took and planted in his field. Though it is the smallest of all seeds, yet when it grows, it is the largest of garden plants and becomes a tree, so that the birds come and perch in its branches" (Matthew 13:31-32). At first, your relationship may be immature and shallow, and your faith

235

may be the size of a mustard seed. But, over time and with nurturance, focus, and investment, your relationship deepens and grows into more than you ever thought it could be (for a mustard seed on its own grows a bush, not a tree), even provided shelter for others.

The second parable compares the Kingdom to preparing dough for baking: "The kingdom of heaven is like yeast that a woman took and mixed into about sixty pounds of flour until it worked all through the dough" (Matthew 13:33). Once again, Jesus is saying what starts comparably small within you spreads throughout every aspect of your life, changing everything. In the Kingdom, the tiniest spark of love is translated into "the richest of fare" (Isaiah 55:2).

A part of this growth process is shedding the old: old habits and behaviors, old preconceptions and interpretations, old beliefs, old values, old understandings of who God is and who you are, even old thoughts on what it means to be married to God. Jesus challenged His disciples to shed the old, once again using parables: "No one sews a patch of unshrunk cloth on an old garment; otherwise, the patch pulls away from it, the new from the old, and the tear becomes worse. And no one pours new wine into old wineskins; otherwise, the wine will burst the skins, and both the wine and the skins will be destroyed. Instead new wine is poured into new wineskins" (Mark 2:21-22). In other words, trying to put something new and fresh on or in something old and well-worn causes damage to both if attempted.

Just prior to sharing these parables, Jesus refers to Himself for the first time as the bridegroom (Mark 2:19-20). Since Jesus moves directly from talking about Himself as the bridegroom to the parables about cloth and wineskins, the ideas are likely related. The old and well-worn in these parables is your old way of life, including your old belief that you can be your own god. Jesus, the bridegroom, is the new cloth and the new wine, but He cannot be sown into your old life or His Spirit poured into your well-worn heart. To do so would cause both a loss of the new (Kingdom life) and damage to the old. You can't make His new paradigm of marriage to Him fit into your old views of life, or both become useless. When you receive your bridegroom, your old life is over. So, you must let go of the old. Anything not belonging to the Kingdom needs to be shed like old, dead skin.

In addition, once the old is shed, you cannot keep looking back to it. As Jesus said, "No one who puts a hand to the plow and looks back is fit for service in the kingdom of God" (Luke 9:62). If you live in the Kingdom, "the old has gone, the new is here" (II Corinthians 5:17). You are to "forget the former things; do not dwell on the past" (Isaiah 43:18). The enemy will try to entice you to look back to the familiar, because the things you are used to are comfortable and easy. However, having a goal of ease and comfort is a value from your old life, and has no place in the Kingdom. Those who live in the Kingdom take the narrow road (Matthew 7:14).

Finally, to live in the Kingdom means being fully committed to the Kingdom life. You can't live with one foot in the Kingdom and one foot in the world. To attempt such a feat divides your heart and mind. As Jesus observed, "if a house is divided against itself, that house cannot stand" (Mark 3:25). Of the double-minded, James 1:8 says they are "unstable in all they do." Straddling the fence won't work. You will fall off, and the side you will land on will be the worldly side.

You can't be sort of married; you either are or you aren't. Marriage is a covenant relationship where you give your whole self to the other and promise fidelity. The same is true of your union with Jesus. You can't be one with Jesus and share your heart with the things of the world, "for what do righteousness and wickedness have in common? Or what fellowship can light have with darkness? What agreement is there between the temple of God and idols? For we are the temple of the living God" (II Corinthians 6:14, 16). You don't have to carve figures out of wood and stone to worship idols. When you put anything above your union with Jesus and your Kingdom life, you are committing spiritual adultery. To live the Kingdom life requires being all in for Jesus.

Speaking about idolatry, Isaiah 17:10-11 declares, "You have forgotten God your Savior; you have not remembered the Rock, your fortress. Therefore, though you set out the finest plants and plant imported vines, though on the day you set them out, you make them grow, and on the morning when you plant them, you bring them to bud, yet the harvest will be as nothing." As the parable of the sower shows, what you plant in your heart determines the fruit you will produce and the harvest you will reap. If you mix in weeds with the seeds of relationship with Jesus, those weeds will choke out the good seeds, and your harvest will be as nothing.

So, living in the Kingdom means faithfulness to one and only one partner as your first love. It means putting aside the enticements of the world and of darkness and loving the light. It means shedding your old skin and all the old ways and beliefs that went along with the old self, receiving the new, and not looking back. Living the Kingdom life is being fully immersed and fully one with Jesus.

CHARACTERISTICS OF THE KINGDOM LIFE

Jesus says you must enter the Kingdom as a little child (Mark 10:15). Several characteristics distinguish little children from grownups. First, little children don't know anything and don't pretend to know anything. They look with wonder at everything, because everything they see is new to them, and every new thing they learn is exciting and amazing. They don't mind their dependency on their parent, but instead welcome it. They are open and trusting and free with giving their love. Unlike adults, with divided loyalties and questionable commitments, children have an unwavering devotion to and faith in their parents. These are the qualities you need for your Kingdom life.

When a little child is learning to walk, she doesn't look at the floor or the obstacles surrounding her. She fixes her eyes on her father, whose outstretched hands are ready to catch her in an instant. The child keeps their eyes on her father until she reaches his loving arms. In the same way, you are to fix your eyes on Jesus (Hebrews 12:2), trust Him with all of you, and find your place of rest in His loving arms. This is why Jesus says the Kingdom belongs to those as little children (Mark 10:14).

Jesus taught the importance of other characteristics in receiving the Kingdom life as God's child and seeing His face, including being poor in spirit (Matthew 5:3), being contrite and lowly in spirit (Isaiah 57:15), being pure in heart (Matthew 5:8), being peacemakers (Matthew 5:9), and being persecuted for righteousness (Matthew 5:10). What does He mean by each of these characteristics and how are they evidenced in your life?

When you are poor, lowly, and contrite in spirit, you recognize your deep need of God. You are very aware you fall far short of God's holiness, and without His grace you would be lost. You gain your esteem from God rather than self, based on who God says you are instead of who you try to be in your own power. You recognize your inability to handle anything on your own, so you rely on God's presence, help, and direction to walk through your life. You understand that staying on the narrow road (Matthew 7:13-14) requires more than your own expertise can pull off without a guide.

You accept that the enemy of God, a spiritual being, is more cunning and much more powerful than you are as a human being, and you recognize you are standing in the middle of a war zone day-in and day-out, ill-equipped to fight alone. Most of all, you realize your brokenness, your woundedness, and your need for healing, and you know you don't have the wisdom to heal yourself.

You are pure in heart when you exchange self as god for dependence on God. You open your heart to His presence each and every moment. You focus on Jesus as the center of your life, fixing your eyes on Him and on nothing else (Hebrews 12:2). You don't see your circumstances but instead look into His face.

You are a peacemaker when you allow the peace of Christ to guard your heart and your mind (Philippians 4:7). You have an expectation of being at peace because you are always in His presence. His peace becomes a bubble enveloping you, and anything that attempts to disrupt His peace bubble, such as the enemy pushing against your peace with a lie, is recognized immediately and addressed with His truth. As a result, His peace remains in place and flows from you into every circumstance you experience, no matter how difficult or painful, which impacts the spiritual realm as well as the world.

To be persecuted for your righteousness, your difference – your new creation and new way of living – must be in evidence to those in your sphere, so much so it would prompt a response from them. This doesn't mean being "holier than thou" or lording your righteousness over others; far from it. In fact, if you feel you must point it out or boast about it, you are not very righteous at all. As Paul said, "May I never boast except in the cross of our Lord Jesus Christ, through which the world has been crucified to me, and I to the world" (Galatians 6:14). No, it means instead others see something in you they both desire and admire, and that your love is so profound and freely given, without fear or self-defense, it impacts others and draws them to Christ.

Persecution, which may take the form of rejection and condemnation or may be more severe, such as accusation, threats, and even imprisonment in some regions, comes from fear in the persecutor. Again, if you respond to their fear with genuine love, you reflect the heart of Christ. Yours is the Kingdom of God.

Finally, Jesus taught a heart of service is a characteristic of living in the Kingdom, by saying, "Come, you who are blessed by my Father; take your inheritance, the kingdom prepared for you since the creation of the world. For I was hungry and you gave me something to eat, I was thirsty and you gave me something to drink, I was a stranger and you invited me in, I needed clothes and you clothed me, I was sick and you looked after me, I was in prison and you came to visit me.' Then the righteous will answer him, 'Lord, when did we see you hungry and feed you, or thirsty and give you something to drink? When did we see you a stranger and invite you in, or needing clothes and clothe you? When did we see you sick or in prison and go to visit you?' The King will reply, 'Truly I tell you, whatever you did for one of the least of these brothers and sisters of mine, you did for me'" (Matthew 25:34-40).

Service done from a sense of obligation grows from a false motive, which means the soil is not good soil and the fruit will not be good fruit. However, service, genuinely offered from a heart of love, grows from deep roots in good soil, and its fruit matches the root. Also, the service needs to allow for the expression of your true self, again keeping the actions grounded in good soil. So, as an example, if you are a gifted cook who loves the experience of sharing meals with others, serving food to the homeless might be a wonderful act of service to express your gifts and your heart. However, if you hate cooking and have no interest in serving food or sharing meals, forcing yourself to serve meals to the homeless because it is a mission at your church won't produce the fruit you intend. Choose instead to serve others in a way that matches your gifts and your heart, always being your true self.

LIVING IN THE KINGDOM

Having established a strong foundation for your Kingdom home in Christ, you can now access all the treasures of the Kingdom and incorporate those treasures into your daily experience. As Paul described in I Timothy 6:19, as you and Jesus partner to build your Kingdom life, you "lay up treasure for (yourself) as a firm foundation for the coming age, so that (you) may take hold of the life that is truly life." Again, in Colossians 2:2-3, Paul talks

242

about being "encouraged in heart and united in love, so that (you) may have the full riches of complete understanding, in order that (you) may know the mystery of God, namely, Christ, in whom are hidden all the treasures of wisdom and knowledge." He goes on to say, "just as you received Christ Jesus as Lord, continue to live your lives in him, rooted and built up in him, strengthened in the faith as you were taught, and overflowing with thankfulness" (Colossians 2:6-7).

With your foundation built on Christ and the roots of your life immersed in Him, you can claim His treasures. With His help, you can begin to live from your true, God-given identity, because you know who He is and who He says you are. Your identity, which reflects aspects of God's nature, can then flow freely into the world, showing Christ and His Kingdom to others, and in your sphere of influence, you usher in His Kingdom by revealing Jesus wherever you go, just by being your best true self.

You can reclaim your authority from the usurping hands of the enemy, making your own choices in partnership with Christ. Because God chose to share His authority with you, you are able to love God, yourself, and others, because love by definition must be freely offered as a gift. You are also able to reject the deceptions and temptations of the enemy, because he can't "make" you do or feel anything against your choice. As you make your life choices, you have ownership of your choices, but you are not responsible or held accountable for the choices of others, so you are never left powerless, having responsibility without any authority to make a different choice. And your choices matter, because through your choices made in partnership with Jesus and following His will, you further His Kingdom.

Through the indwelling of His Spirit in your heart, you are made one with Jesus and take on His likeness more and more. Your spirit can take leadership over your flesh. The presence of His Spirit brings you the richness and depth of a heart filled with love, joy, and peace, and these grow into the fruit of patience, kindness, gentleness, and goodness toward others. In addition, His Spirit strengthens your faith and helps you exhibit balance and restraint. As a result, you are able to respond in a thoughtful and loving way, instead of reacting out of your own flesh and woundedness. In addition, His spiritual gifts prepare you to fight the battle for His Kingdom as it comes into the world and assist you in building up others in their fight for His Kingdom.

Christ's protection over your spirit provides you with peace to guard your heart and mind, such that any disruption to His peace warns you immediately of an enemy attack. He also offers you a full armament for battle, covering you and equipping you to fight the enemy effectively. His truth wards off all lies, bringing healing to your heart for past wounds and shielding your heart from new injury. Jesus also brings redemption, turning for good even those things Satan intends for evil and restoring what has been stolen. Because you are able to live in a bubble of His peace, shielded and defended by Him, the Kingdom can flourish in you and flow freely from you into the world.

Jesus also gives you confidence before the throne of God, because through His blood, you are sanctified. You know you are made pure and holy and blameless. All the evidence the enemy has stacked against you is excluded, thrown out, never to be presented in court. Satan can make no accusation or claim against you, ever again. Shame is demolished; fear has no place in you. You are made perfect in spirit, not because of what you have done, but because of His work on the cross and His cleansing of your sin. Because of His sanctification, you can grow in faith and spiritual maturity, becoming His treasure, in much the same way He gives you His treasures.

Through knowing God, you gain wisdom. His wisdom helps you discern the presence of evil and distinguish good from evil, to discern inner qualities, and to have insight and good judgment. Through His eyes, you can see beyond the superficial, beneath the surface to the process level of understanding to discern the deeper movements and meanings of life. Satan's fake offerings are revealed for what they are. The more wisdom you gain, the more you realize how little you know, and the more your reverence for God deepens; the more your reverence grows, the more wisdom you gain. The "wisdom" of the world begins to look like foolishness, the things of the world begin to dim and fade from view, and your focus shifts to things of import and eternal significance. Your Kingdom house is built up by the hands of the Master Craftsman in a manner that will stand through all storms, so you can abide and rest in the arms of the Lord for all eternity.

Now, you can live free. Your debt is paid. Jesus has exchanged Himself as ransom for your freedom. Your captor is now captive. You are free from the law, free from judgment, and free from slavery to sin. His truth sets you free and keeps you free from the enemy's lies about who you are and who God is, so you are free from fear and shame. You are free to live from your true heart, being your true best self, living your life to the fullest, and allowing transforming love to flow freely from you. You are free to be God's child, receiving the abundance of His full inheritance, standing as co-heir with Christ before God. As God's child, you are free to be a full partner with Jesus, moving and flowing through life together as one. And this is Kingdom living.

CONCLUSION

How is the soil of your heart? Is it dry and hardened? Disconnected and shallow? Stony, thick, and gritty? Choked with weeds? Or will you allow Jesus to plow and prepare your heart to be His home? Have you shed the old and allowed Him to bring the new? Do you look back to the past and your old ways, or do you keep your eyes fixed on Jesus (Hebrews 12:2)? Have you been made like a little child, pure in spirit, humble and loving in heart? Will you sell all you own to purchase the field, now that you know the treasure buried within it? Will you sell all you own to purchase the pearl of greatest value? Are you ready to receive in full the treasures of living in His Kingdom now?

As C. S. Lewis said, "At the end of things, the Blessed will say, 'We have never lived anywhere except in Heaven.' And the lost will say, 'We were always in Hell.' And both will speak truly."[3] Where will you choose to live?

The book has come full circle now, tying together all of the treasures to offer you a picture of the Kingdom life. As you reach its end, I pray the treasure map contained within these pages plants good seeds to help you join in partnership with Jesus, build a strong foundation in Him, and seek the treasures of a Kingdom life. I will end with Paul's exhortation: "Finally, brothers and sisters, whatever is true, whatever is noble, whatever is right, whatever is pure, whatever is lovely, whatever is admirable – if anything is excellent or praiseworthy – think about such things" (Philippians 4:8). These are the things of His Kingdom.

Starting Point: Questions on Kingdom Living

Answer the following questions to further seek the Kingdom of God. Consider your answers prayerfully and thoughtfully. Don't offer a superficial response and move on to the next question but look deeply within and be as honest with yourself as you can be. Avoid giving "pat" answers you might have heard in church, particularly if you've not examined what those responses mean in depth. These questions are designed to further help you uncover the treasures of His Kingdom, so you can experience living in His Kingdom now.

1. As God's soldier behind enemy lines, part of His invading force, what is your assignment to help usher in His Kingdom?
2. What is the current status of the soil of your heart? What do you need Jesus to do to prepare your ground for planting? How can you partner with Him to accomplish the preparation of your heart?
3. In what ways have you made lies your refuge and falsehoods your hiding place?
4. To continue your training, what spiritual disciplines do you desire to implement in your life? Which ones seem to work best for you?
5. How has God used your mistakes and hardships you have experienced in your life to develop your spiritual maturity?

6. What lies do you need removed from your garden and replaced by God's truth? What is the status of your "self as god" lie?
7. What old habits, old behaviors, old thoughts and beliefs, old values, old perceptions and old ways do you need to shed?
8. What idols do you have that interfere with your faithfulness to your true partner? What do you need to give up or let go of to be fully wed to Christ?
9. Which characteristics of the Kingdom life do you possess? What do you need to receive from Jesus to gain the characteristics of the Kingdom life you do not yet have?
10. Looking at the complete list of Kingdom treasures, which treasures have you purchased? Which ones do you need to seek and purchase?

DESTINATION: PRAYERS FOR KINGDOM LIVING

Find a quiet place with few distractions to sit with Jesus. Still your mind and quiet your heart by repeating a verse of Scripture meaningful to you; for example, you could repeat, "seek his kingdom, and these things will be given to you" (Luke 12:31). I have written a prayer for you as an example, but use your own words, from your heart, to ask Jesus to seek His Kingdom: *Lord, you tell me you want to plow the soil of my heart and plant yourself, your word, your truth, and your life within me. Would you please show me what needs to be cleared away and what needs to be pulled out to make room for your planting? I am willing, Lord, for you to do as you will to ready my heart and implant your Kingdom within me. Please take my willingness as my choice and do what you need to do to prepare me. As I open my heart to you, would you tell me what you want to do and how I can be your partner in accomplishing the good work you are finishing in me?*

After you pray, spend time in silent meditation, eyes closed and listening for His answers. He may show you an image in your mind, or you may hear words or phrases in your mind, or you may sense emotions or experiences He brings to you to help you experience His Kingdom. He also might bring to mind a particular verse or story from Scripture to further explain His Kingdom and prepare the ground of your heart for His seeds. You can recognize responses from the Lord by the peace they stir up in your heart. If an image or word comes to you that brings anxiety or shame, reject it, recenter yourself on Jesus, and ask again. If you think you hear a response that contradicts Scripture, pray against enemy interference, recenter on Jesus, and ask again. Otherwise, don't analyze what comes up or question if it's the Lord. Instead, go with it and follow wherever He takes you. If you are getting "off base," He will let you know. Keep with it, asking Jesus to explain anything you don't understand and to show you more, until you feel He is finished.

If you don't hear anything, don't be concerned or frustrated. Remember, we have an enemy who actively opposes our treasure seeking and tries to thwart our relationship with Jesus. Take a break and come back to your prayer later. This time, if you don't receive a response, ask Jesus what is in the way. It may be a lie you believe, blocking you from experiencing His Kingdom, such as you aren't worthy to receive His Kingdom. You may be unaware you are agreeing with the enemy and your own agreement is getting in your way. Ask Jesus for discernment to identify any hindrances to what He wants to do in you that you may have agreed to accept from the enemy. Whatever Jesus reveals is in the way, ask Him to bring truth to your heart to move the hindrance out of your way. Then return to your prayer request.

Another prayer you could pursue involves seeking the treasures of the Kingdom and receiving them in full. An example of this type of prayer could be: *Lord, I desire to know my true identity, to reclaim the authority you have given me, to experience your indwelling Spirit, to receive your protection and sanctification, to gain your wisdom, and to know your freedom. Would you reveal each of these treasures to me in such a way that I experience them to their fullest expression? I ask you to remove anything from the enemy that is in the way of receiving your treasures, and I ask you create in me the kind of heart ready to live in your Kingdom. Would you show me what you need to do in me and help me to respond by faith? What would you like to show me about each one of these treasures you offer?* This prayer may need to be broken down into seven individual prayers, each seeking one of the specific treasures. You can go back to prayers from earlier chapters to help you seek each treasure more fully. You can also look back over answers you have received from Him during previous prayers to recall truths He has brought to your heart. Ask Him to bring these concepts and understandings together into a whole, complete picture of His Kingdom within you.

Finally, you can ask Jesus to remove idols and to help you shed your old preconceptions of God, of yourself, of life, of the world, and of His Kingdom, to be replaced with truth. This type of prayer might be: *Lord, I don't want anything to clutter my house that is not of your Kingdom. Would you please show me any idols I have that are taking parts of my love and focus off of you and help me to put them down? Would you show me what old perceptions, old thoughts, old beliefs, old behaviors, old values, old interpretations, old feelings, and old understandings I need to shed? Please show me how those old ways are causing me harm and, as I am willing, help me to let them go.*

Always remember to listen as you pray and remain open to whatever He wants to show you or wherever He wants to take you. Intimacy at this level can be scary, but He is a good and loving Father who wants only good for you. If you know this, or if He can show you this through prayer, you won't be afraid to open your heart to Him completely.

As always, don't try to figure out the answers yourself. Remember, for Jesus, everything is about the relationship, including living in the Kingdom. In fact, the Kingdom life is relationship. His love is the basis of every Kingdom treasure you seek. Allow yourself to experience the height and depth and width and length of His love for you. As you come to know the riches of His love, you will receive the treasures of His Kingdom.

SETTING THE COURSE: LIVING IN HIS KINGDOM

The first section presents concepts you may want to internalize, and the second section lists some actions you may take to apply the information you have studied. Approach the following concepts and actions prayerfully. Avoid any thinking that you must rigidly adhere to them, because these are only suggestions and may not work for you. Everyone is different. Remember, the Kingdom life is a gift of God, and living in His Kingdom isn't something you can accomplish but is established through partnership with Christ.

Use these suggestions to deepen your relationship with Him in your quest to live the Kingdom life.

INTERNALIZE THE CONCEPTS

Consider the significance of the statement: your eternal life has already begun. Meditate on His presence within you. Contemplate what kinds of treasures His presence brings to you and what those treasures mean to you.

Examine your battle between your flesh and your spirit. Consider the consequences of this battle in your life. Explore what it means to allow your spirit to take preeminence over the flesh.

Meditate on the state of being of the soil of your heart. Examine the nature of your weeds. Consider if you have buried your heart or hidden it away. Examine the rocks that may be cluttering your ground. Contemplate the process of clearing and plowing your ground to ready you for planting.

Explore the growth process of your relationship with Jesus from its inception. Consider both how far you have come and how far you need to go to experience the fullness of the Kingdom life. Examine what you hold onto that still needs to be shed. Contemplate the kind of partner you make, including your fidelity and commitment to the relationship.

Meditate on the imagery of learning to walk as a little child. Visualize yourself as a child walking toward your Father and falling into His loving arms.

Meditate on each of the Kingdom treasures: your identity, your authority, His indwelling Spirit, His protection, His sanctification, His wisdom, and your freedom in Christ. Consider the state of each treasure in your life. Explore with Jesus areas needing growth and expansion for each of the treasures.

Contemplate the C. S. Lewis quote: "At the end of things, the Blessed will say, 'We have never lived anywhere except in Heaven.' And the lost will say, 'We were always in Hell.' And both will speak truly." Consider the deeper meanings and significance of his words. Meditate on your choice of where you will live your eternal life.

PROCESS THEIR APPLICATION

Create a painting, drawing, collage of photographs, or meme that describes the present state of your heart's soil. Save what you've created but keep it readily accessible, somewhere you can see it. As you process and pray about Jesus plowing and planting your garden, change the picture to reflect the changes you experience in the state of your heart. Keep altering and expanding your image of your field, until you are satisfied the picture reflects a Kingdom life. You can then hang or post your creation to remind you of how Jesus has worked in your heart.

Remember back to your childhood, to your earliest memories. Close your eyes and revisit those memories, noticing the qualities your child-self possesses. Try to feel the heart of that little child – its humility, innocence, and faith. Notice also any characteristics you see in this little child. Is the child a free spirit? A loving heart? A fierce warrior? Gentle? Kind? Compassionate? Caring? Protective? Insightful? Wise beyond their years? Through prayer, ask Jesus to show you how this child reflects your best true self.

Go on a musical Scavenger Hunt, looking for songs whose lyrics reflect the Kingdom treasures discussed in this book. For example, you could search for a song that talks about who Jesus says you are to represent the identity chapter. For the chapter on authority, you could look for lyrics about choosing Jesus, responsibility, or standing against the enemy. The chapter on His indwelling Spirit lends itself to a song about the Holy Spirit's presence, the fruit of the Spirit, or the gifts of the Spirit. For the chapter on His protection, you could look for a song about peace or redemption. A song about holiness, about the cross, or about His covering your sins would be appropriate, and so on for each of the treasures. Once you have found songs you like that represent the treasures to you, listen to them periodically to remind yourself of your Kingdom treasures. Because music activates a different part of your brain than language alone, associating music with your treasures will help you remember and apply what you've learned in the book.

Sketch a map to the Kingdom based on the information provided in each chapter of this book. Use different colors to represent the different treasures. Look for areas of connection and overlap in your treasure map, for there are connecting points and overlapping ideas throughout. Be creative in the way you choose to express the ideas presented in this book, using symbols that have meaning to you. Make the map user-friendly, meaning draw it in a way that makes it useful to you in seeking His Kingdom on an ongoing basis.

Conclusion

Your treasure map is now complete. You have searched the world over for pearls of value, but now you have discovered a priceless pearl, one of such value it cannot be matched. You have found the field where the treasure chest is buried, dug up the treasure, and opened the chest to find it overflowing with jewels of such magnificent beauty words can't describe them, and a wealth of riches impossible to measure. All that is left is for you to decide if you are willing to sell all you own to possess these treasures.

Are you willing to give up your pride, your self-determination, and your belief in the illusion of control? Will you refuse all external measures of your value and worth? Will you put down your self-reliance and self-protection? Will you leave behind your old life, your past sins, and your lie beliefs? Will you release your unforgiveness of yourself and others into the hands of Jesus? Will you put down your shame? Will you stop listening to fear? Are you willing to let go of the sparkling, glittering, cheap jewelry of the world and the costume jewelry of the enemy? Will you exchange the temporary for the eternal?

Your role in seeking His Kingdom is willingness. If you are willing, Jesus will help you through the process. He will walk with you each step of the way, leading you, guiding you, strengthening you, encouraging you, supporting you, carrying you when necessary. But His love for you and the freedom He chose to provide you mandates that He wait on your willing participation.

A young, rich man once approached Jesus, asking for the secrets to the Kingdom of God. This man loved God and followed His commandments, but Jesus said to him that he still lacked one thing and told him to sell all he owned and give to the poor to gain treasure in heaven. Sadly, the young man walked away, because he perceived that he had great wealth (Matthew 19:16-22). In truth, his so-called riches were worthless, but he was unwilling to part with them.

You have the freedom to be like the rich, young man, or to be like Peter, who dropped his nets and his livelihood, and left everything from his old life behind to follow Jesus. The choice is yours. Will you follow the map to the treasures of the Kingdom and sell all you have to possess them? I hope this book will help you along your way on your greatest adventure, and I pray for you as Paul prayed: "I keep asking that the God of our Lord Jesus Christ, the glorious Father, may give you the Spirit of wisdom and revelation, so that you may know him better. I pray that the eyes of your heart may be enlightened in order that you may know the hope to which he has called you, the riches of his glorious inheritance in his holy people, and his incomparably great power for us who believe" (Ephesians 1:17-19). Amen.

Definitions

Agency: personal authority over yourself, your body, your thoughts, your emotions, your choices, your actions, your responses, your feelings; the individual capacity to act independently and make your own free choices.

Authority: the right to make decisions and direct someone or something.

Choice: the act of making a decision between two or more possibilities.

Control: the power to direct events and determine outcomes.

Faith: being fully persuaded of a belief such that you trust it without doubt, and your actions reflect your belief.

Freedom: the right to choose without hindrance or restraint, absent any subjugation, imprisonment, or enslavement; the unimpeded expression of your true identity, without interference; the unrestricted expression of your authority.

Identity: your inner qualities; the unique, intrinsic characteristics of your nature; the essence of your being.

Indwell: to abide within, as a guiding force, or to inhabit.

Protection: presence during difficulty; shielding; preserving.

Sanctify: to set apart and declare as holy, to consecrate as sacred and dedicated to God, to purify and cleanse free from sin, to approve, and to exculpate or declare not guilty of wrongdoing.

Sovereign: having the right to reign; having the authority to establish the foundations, structures, and laws for a kingdom.

Wisdom: the ability to discern inner traits, having insight, and having the qualities of experience, knowledge, and good judgment.

Resources

[1]Lewis, C. S. (1970). *God in the Dock: Essays on Theology and Ethics.* Cambridge, U.K.: Eerdmans Publishing Company.

[2]Lewis, C. S. (1952). *Mere Christianity.* New York: HarperCollins.

[3]Lewis, C. S. (1946) *The Great Divorce.* New York: HarperCollins.

Other Titles by This Author

NONFICTION:

  Strength in Adversity

  Strength in Our Story

  Wilderness Meditations

  Trauma Narrative Treatment

  Restored Christianity

  Please Share the Door, I'm Freezing: Creating Oneness in
      Marriage

  Ready to Learn

FICTION:

  Sky Light Rises: Whisperers Book Two

  Sky Light Falls: Whisperers Book One

  The Interview

CHILDREN'S BOOKS:

  Where is God?

  Gold Stone

  God Knows All About You

www.ingramcontent.com/pod-product-compliance
Lightning Source LLC
LaVergne TN
LVHW041212080426
835508LV00011B/927

9781732811270